Fiction As Truth

The Author in 1928

Fiction As Truth

Selected Literary Writings
by
Richard Hughes

Edited and Introduced by
Richard Poole

POETRY WALES PRESS
1983

PUBLISHED BY POETRY WALES PRESS
56 PARCAU AVENUE, BRIDGEND, MID GLAMORGAN

First Impression 1983

British Library Cataloguing in Publication Data

Hughes Richard, *1900-1971*
   Fiction as truth.
   1. Hughes, Richard – Criticism and interpretation
   I. Title   II. Poole, Richard
   823'.8   PR6015.U35

   ISBN 0-907476-18-X

The publisher acknowledges the financial assistance of the Welsh Arts Council.

TYPESET BY AFAL, CARDIFF
PRINTED IN 11pt BASKERVILLE II
BY
D. BROWN & SONS LIMITED,
BRIDGEND, MID GLAMORGAN.

Contents

Introduction

Plainly, there are always two good reasons for collecting (or, as in this case, making a selection from) the scattered occasional writings on literature of a famous author – whether during his lifetime, or post-humously: from them a reader may expect to learn something of the author's views on his predecessors and contemporaries, something of the author's approach to his craft. When the collection spans, however, virtually fifty years – virtually the author's writing life – a reader may expect to trace in its contents something more: I mean the growth, maturation, development (call it what you will) of the author's mind. This process is to be found, of course, in his poems, plays, novels, in his "pure" creative works: but it will be no less discernible in a collection of writings done over a lifetime.

Even before he left Oxford, Richard Hughes (born 1900; died 1976) was living the life of a professional literary man – writing poems and stories for magazine publication and reviewing regularly for London journals. (Indeed, his undistinguished degree can hardly have been unconnected with the demands made on his time by his extramural activities.) This early period, anterior to the writing of *A High Wind in Jamaica*, is represented here by the Preface to the poetry, the reviews of W.E. Henley and *Mrs Dalloway*, and the Introduction to the selection of Skelton's poems which Hughes made for Heinemann in 1924. If the last of these betrays an impatience with scholarship that is often to be found in young men, the Henley review (written several years earlier) surely testifies to a precocious critical sensibility. Viewed retrospectively, the Preface and the piece on *Mrs Dalloway* are pregnant with significance for Hughes's imminent practice as a novelist. In his emphases in the Preface upon pattern and idea-images (eidola), one sees him clarifying for his own benefit conceptions that might not only be fruitful in the making of poems but in the making of novels. What, for instance, are the images (for we have here much more than set descriptions) of the octopus in Chapter 7 of *A High Wind in Jamaica* and the propellor-shaft of the *Archimedes* in Chapter 1 of *In Hazard* but eidola? Whilst in the review of *Mrs Dalloway*, Hughes's own prose radiates, not just with life caught up from the novelist he is responding to (a novelist whose example shows that poetic writing need not be alien to the texture of a contemporary novel), but with a sensuous vitality which is his own. Hughes's thinking about poetry and fiction was never discontinuous, as was Robert Graves's (that they disagreed about the relationship between these two kinds of writing, the 'Introduction to *In Hazard*' testifies). When Hughes stopped writing verse in his mid-twenties, he did not turn his back on his poetic talents – rather, they became weapons in his fiction-making armoury.

The contents of this book are divided into four sections. The first contains pieces in which Hughes considers, concurrently or retrospect-ively, his creative work: all four aspects of it are represented – the poetry, the drama, the stories for children, the fiction. The near-thirty year gap between 'Fear and *In Hazard*' (written in the year of the novel's publication) and the 'Introduction' (first published in 1966) is particularly instructive: in the first piece one sees the author, in response to the imperceptive efforts of reviewers, performing a fairly straightforward act of literary criticism on his own novel; in the second the author probing, with mature reflection, the inarticulate unconscious depths in which the book germinated and out of which it sprang. The earlier piece was originally entitled 'Why I wrote *In Hazard*', but it is the later 'Introduction' which really grapples with that question.

In the second section I have placed writings which bear chiefly upon the business of fiction. The version of 'Under the Nose and Under the Skin' I include here is by two years the later of two: the earlier version of 1929, which appeared in the book pages of the *New York Herald Tribune*, was an immediate reaction to an article by Sinclair Lewis. When a would-be Middle West authoress asked Lewis whether it was necessary for her to come to New York and "see the world" in order to have something to write about, Lewis advised her to stay at home and write about what was under her nose. This, with suitable disdain, Hughes dismissed in his American piece as "merest sentimentality":

> It shows as romantic an outlook on the psychological mechanics of writing as if he had told her to take her typewriter up Mount Marcy, where the Great Spirit would produce her 70,000 words by cock crow.

The English version has not the perkiness of the American one, but I have preferred it because its argument seems to me to be both more compact and more considered.

Between 1954 and 1956 Hughes gave twenty lectures, at the rate of four per term, at Gresham College in the University of London as Professor of Rhetoric. Some of these lectures survive complete, some are represented by a few initial pages (or paragraphs) of consecutive prose plus notes, some by skeletal notes alone. For this book I have found it possible only to extract, from the complete text of a lecture of Autumn 1955 entitled 'The Novel behind your Eyes', two brief passages. For this paucity of usable material there are three reasons: first, the fragmentary state of the whole course of lectures; secondly, the fact that, spread thinly over a considerable period as they were, Hughes found it necessary continually to give lengthy recapitulations; and thirdly, the fact that he draws heavily upon the work of other theorists in the field – upon, notably, I.A. Richards and William Empson. From the start Hughes saw rhetoric very much from a writer's angle – his early lectures define it as the art of producing a desired impression in a reader no less than in a listener. Later, however, he came to distinguish between what a writer puts into his writing (''the cerebration resulting *in* a poem''), which he called ''poetic'', and the effect that writing has upon a reader (''the cerebration resulting *from* a poem''), which he called rhetoric proper. Hughes was here, as so often in his thinking, very much on top of his time: in May 1955 he was discussing – and criticizing – conceptions from semantics and metalinguistics. Had he been alive today, he would not have been in the least surprised by (he was a thoroughly unsurprisable man) – would indeed, I think, have taken in his stride – the ideas underlying the edifices of structuralism and post-structuralism.

But the crucial article in this section, and the latest-written in the book, is 'Fiction as Truth'. This piece bears, I believe, the same intimacy of relation to Hughes's two post-war novels as the 'Preface' to the poetry bears to the two pre-war ones. The distinction which it makes between the mystic who opens himself to the ''Other'' and the solipsist who sees himself as the only reality in a world of his own articulation is explored in *The Human Predicament* through the diametrically-opposed figures of Mitzi von Kessen, the blind nun, and the dictator Adolf Hitler. 'Fiction as Truth' is the quintessential statement of a liberal humanist in life as well as art, and is, I think, deserving of classic status. Nearly fifty years before, a more devil-may-care Hughes could write, on the tension between aesthetic and moral considerations in a work of art (in an unsent letter to Amabel Williams-Ellis):

> There is the ordinary moral "ought" and the aesthetic "ought": you can say that an artist "ought" to have used more red, less green, where there is plainly no moral significance. Now: if there are two "oughts" why should they not clash: why "ought" not the artist to draw a curve, so, while at the same time he "ought" to be feeding his wife, and so? And if two "oughts" can clash – for there can be no balancing of pros and cons when there is a definite difference in kind: you can't value acts of parliament in relation to glue – if they clash, where is Kant's Categorical Imperative? Nursing its shins somewhere in the Ewigkeit, I am afraid: there is no absolute standard of right and wrong, and Morality has to pass down the car.

Over the years Hughes's aestheticism negotiated a *modus vivendi* with his awareness of ethical imperatives – the process may be studied in and through the four novels – until, towards the end of his life, at a time when many younger novelists were once more valuing, in their fictions, aesthetic considerations above moral ones, the determinedly post-Darwinian and post-Freudian author of *A High Wind in Jamaica* bore not a little of the air of a nineteenth-century Tolstoyan sage. Lover of irony and paradox though he was, however, one can be in no doubt that in 'Fiction as Truth' Hughes is saying the most important thing he knows, a truth to which a lifetime's experience as man and artist testifies, and a truth he believes civilised humankind ignores at its peril.

The third section brings together four talks: three lectures and a short broadcast. Hughes wrote and broadcast repeatedly about Wales and Welsh affairs throughout his lifetime and his plays and fiction show that he could write of what was "under his nose" as well as what was "under his skin". I have included 'Nationalism and Literature' as the most wide-ranging reflection of his thoughts of around 1930 on the character of Welsh culture. Forty years on, he could not speak so buoyantly about the state of ethnic music in Welsh homes:

> A Greek geographer in the fifth century BC commented on our fondness for the harp, and for hymn-singing in our "curious round temples"; in the Middle Ages, Giraldus tried hard to describe to an England still ignorant of musical harmony the strange Welsh invention of part-singing, which even Welsh children seemed able to do from the cradle – but today it is all laid on by the BBC. Seldom now on a Sunday are there

chapel walls bursting with those tremendous tenors and baritones and basses who used to set the whole stone building quivering like a sound-box. And those long winter evenings once spent with a harpist and a group of neighbours singing at the farmhouse fireside: they are all too busy nowadays watching the telly.

'You should have been here yesterday'

Still, in a lecture given at the University College of North Wales in 1974 entitled 'Wales as a Writer's Habitat', he felt able to defend the dispersed against the centralized culture, to speak of "the Great Metropolitan Fallacy, which demands for every country one Capital City drawing to itself all the best brains of every generation – and the devil take the provinces". In this talk he makes it plain that, from the time during his schooldays when he visited Robert Graves in Harlech, to the years spent in Laugharne with Dylan Thomas as his neighbour and Vernon Watkins and Augustus John among his many and frequent visitors, to his last home – Môr Edrin, which looks across the Dwyryd Estuary to Portmeirion, Wales gave him "the best of all possible worlds":

> An ineffable beauty, fresh to me just when the sensitive eyes of youth needed it most, yet coupled with return to the homeland where all my atavistic emotional roots lay. A beauty of which even the eyes of old age could never tire. Co-habitants, quite different from myself yet fundamentally with the same kind of values. And the solitude of a desert hermitage, alternating with a hive of intellectual ferment that recalled the great days of the Mermaid Tavern.

The other pieces in this section illustrate Hughes's long involvement with radio-broadcasting, his informed interest (not often to be found in artists) in physical science, and his practical participation as a lay Christian (and a skilled user of words) in the ongoing life of the Church. 'The Voice and the Pen' is closely related to two near-identical articles on literature and radio which appeared in 1946 and 1947, but does not, as they do, overlap significantly with 'The Birth of Radio Drama' of ten years later.

The fourth and last section gathers pieces on books and authors. It draws mainly on the large number of reviews produced by Hughes during more than fifty years of literary journalism, but also includes his Introduction to his 1924 selection from the poems of Skelton, his centenary broadcast tribute to R.L. Stevenson, the *Radio Times* article published on the occasion of the first broadcast of his play for voices *Nowhere at Home*, on George Borrow, and, last of all, a brief contribution to the literary history of the early part of the century on what may be thought the unlikely championship of one famous novelist by another. I shall not labour this section beyond suggesting that it is interesting to compare what Hughes says of *Wild Wales* in this piece of 1954 with what he said of it thirty years earlier in an article entitled 'Wales and the Welsh'. He submits there that the Cultured Englishman who has gained his knowledge of the Welsh through Borrow's *Wild Wales* and Caradoc Evans's *My People* is unlikely to be well-informed:

> the first is spoiled by an excessively imaginative romanticism, which colours everything the colour of Borrow's own mind, the second is a cold-blooded and wilful trading on English ignorance, prompted by personal dislike of his fellow-countrymen, and having at most only a local application to one or two valleys.

If Hughes's attitude to *My People* did not subsequently soften, his attitude to *Wild Wales* did, and he came to understand Borrow with a typically Hughesian complexity. Having proposed and rejected as tempting but inadequate the idea that there was no real Borrow, the idea that the multi-faceted Borrow of the books is a self-creation, the Narrator of *Nowhere at Home* in his concluding statement suggests that Borrow's ''root incompatibility'' arose from there being two souls in his body, the soul of a man of letters and the soul of a man of action:

> unless both souls were satisfied, they tended to tear at and frustrate each other. Only once were they both equally employed – in Spain, *The Bible in Spain*. In Wales – a walking tour, however strenuous, is hardly ''action''. *Lavengro, The Romany Rye* . . . the gaps in *time* between the experience and the recounting of it was perhaps too wide, so that instead of galloping authentic Arab stallions we find him sometimes galloping . . . hobby-horses.

Hughes's many-faceted Borrow and his onion-like T.E. Lawrence complement one another: did Hughes find in these men something of his own complexity?

I began this Introduction by suggesting that in these writings may be traced the growth of a mind. It seems to me no less true that they provide evidence that, having come to certain conclusions, having formulated certain ideas – indeed, *idea-images* – Hughes remained faithful to them throughout his life. A notable eidolon is that of the hen and its egg. This metaphor for the relationship between the artist and his creation, first elaborated in the Preface to the poetry, appears eleven years afterwards in 'Under the Nose and Under the Skin' and a further thirty-five years on in the 'Introduction to *In Hazard*'. Subtly adjusted, it appears in the review of *Under Milk Wood* as a phoenix egg which tends to burn the bird which lays it; and in a part of the Gresham lectures not reproduced here, Hughes employed the notion of a *cuckoo's* egg when speaking of the writer who must lay his egg to be hatched in the borrowed nest of the reader's mind.

Now an editor's technical notes. 'On *The Human Predicament*', like 'Literature and the Plastic Arts' and 'Why do we read Novels?', is an extract from a longer piece, a broadcast of 1961 called 'A Writer and his Times'. 'A Preface to his Poetry' is composite in nature: in the main it consists of an unpublished Preface of late 1921 or early 1922, but this has been expanded with material from a closely-related lecture, 'Technique of Poetry', belonging to the same period. 'A Preface to his Poetry' was first published in *Poetry Wales* in Winter 1981. Several items appear in print here for the first time: 'Fear and *In Hazard*', 'On *The Human Predicament*', the two pieces comprising 'The Novel behind your Eyes', 'The Poet and the Scientist', 'The Voice and the Pen'. I have not been able to discover the occasion of the lecture 'The Poet and the Scientist', but I guess that it was given in the 1930s. In editing this collection of lectures, broadcasts, articles and reviews, I have been conscious that differences exist between what was written for the eye and what for the ear; but I have contented myself with making only such cuts and alterations as seemed desirable in presenting pieces some of whose original occasions were far removed in kind from the present one.

Finally I wish to thank Peter Thomas and John Jenkins, who gave bibliographical aid, and Lucy McEntee – without whose enthusiastic co-operation this book would not have got off the ground.

Richard Poole
August 1982

I
Autobiographical

A Preface to his Poetry

Critics like Prefaces, for a certain reason: and the Gentle Reader
generally skips them: so I make no apology for adressing myself to the
analytical rather than to the amateur, the appreciative mind. It may be
taken as a confession of weakness that an author's faith should not be
sufficiently justified by his works alone, but should need some sort of a
poetical Athanasian Creed to support it: and so I admit it to be: I should
not have meditated a Preface at all if it were not that the recent
experiment of publishing six pieces in an anthology provoked such a
higgledy-piggledy of verdicts as "Blows iridescent word-bubbles", and
"Has a queer, uncouth power, but should not imitate Browning's
worst lines!" But if one of the functions of criticism is to discover what
an author is trying to do before debating the matter of his success, surely
the critic should not cavil at a practice manifestly intended to ease his
task. On the other hand, when I set myself to the composition of some
sort of explanatory introduction I found it exceedingly difficult: I felt
like the Russian dancer who was asked What It All Meant, and replied
"If I could tell you, do you think I would put myself to the infinite pains
of dancing it?" Consequently this Preface has shaped itself more into a
rather disjointed essay on the nature and technique of poetry in general
than a particular apology. For although these are my present views,
they were not my opinions when I wrote most of the verse in this book,
which consists of juvenilia, really, covering for the most part the last
four years of my minority, when I cannot pretend to have held any
conscious opinions at all. Most theories are retrospective; for the
purposes of actual composition they are, of course, quite damning. But
if the critic should complain that it is an unnecessary piece of arrogance
to print a Preface at all in that case, I would remind him that the
publication of anything presumes a certain arrogance, and that a little
excess of it is neither here nor there.

I believe that there is not, and never can be, any single holy catholic
faith in poetics: that the phenomenon of poetry cannot be traced to any

single source, any more than the Universe or Truth can be reduced to any single principle. I must confess to being a polytheist both in religion and art. As for these psychological sources, there may be dozens of them, all quite distinct from each other: but it is the usual habit of theorists to insist upon one source to the exclusion of all the rest. For my present purposes I will only refer to three: and probably the easiest way of tackling them will be to reduce each to a plausible though inexact definition of Man.

Mr. Robert Graves' theory, as expressed in his imminent book *On English Poetry,* depends on Man as a Neurotic Animal. Starting from Professor Rivers' developments of modern psychological theory, he argues that poetry is to the poet what dreams are to the ordinary man; a symbolical way, that is, of resolving those complexes which deadlock of emotion have produced: but with this difference, that while dreams resolve a man's private neuroses only, it is the universal nature of poetry to be able to resolve the reader's too: a psycho-therapeutist, in fact, might set up with the Oxford Book of English Verse as his sole dispensary. This is certainly a most important discovery: it is one of the truest and therefore most dangerous discoveries in the recent history of literary criticism – most dangerous, because when all is said and done Truth is the only effective weapon against itself. No wholly false theory ever did damage to a true one: it is when Truth meets Truth that there comes the tug-of-war. It is a curious, but inevitable quality of the Universe, that when two truths meet they almost invariably fight as fiercely as two Kilkenny cats. It is obviously premature to criticise Graves' thesis; indeed, I hope I am committing no breach of etiquette in referring to it at all. Criticism will come soon enough, when a vast army shall have arisen, calling themselves Metamorphic Poets, taking Graves as their Bible and each writing worse poetry than the last. That will not be Graves' fault: it will be inevitable. They would have written bad poetry anyhow: but if it had not been for the Divine Sanction of Metamorphism, it would probably never have seen the light. Then Metamorphism will be the bugbear, the idol to be broken up and carted away. But it will be none the less true, for all that.

All I would suggest is this: that psycho-therapy is the greatest discovery of the modern mind: and that at present it is only natural that it should assume importance over the heads of all other discoveries of the human mind that there ever have been. But in time it will be reduced to a position of proper perspective among them: and then, and not till then, will Graves' theory be put in proper perspective among the other sources of the phenomenon of poetry.

The next definition which I would propose is founded upon Aristotle's: I would vary his πολιτικον ζῷον by calling Man a Communicative Animal. To say that he has a natural impulse towards self-expression is inadequate, and has led to a good many heresies: for one cannot express oneself *in vacuo:* one has to express something to someone else. Expression must be intelligible to others beside the artist: and a poem which is only intelligible to its poet is not merely regrettable from the point of view of the rest of the world, it is inadequate from the author's own point of view: it would simply be a farce to call it self-expression. If it should be argued that this communicative instinct, which although it differentiates man from brute with greater truth than Aristotle's political instinct, is not sufficiently fundamental to merit exaltation into a definition, I would reply that it is a foundation of all knowledge and all art: that knowledge is the receptive aspect of communicativeness, and art the productive, the inside and outside of the jacket. For if the sole function of poetry were to resolve of the jacket. For if the sole function of poetry were to resolve the poet's neuroses, there would be no earthly need for him to show his poems to anyone else – presuming, of course, that he is not a professional psycho-therapeutist: and yet that poet is not yet born who was content to put his poems in the fire as soon as he had written them. Instinct tells him that it is as much his function to publish his poems as it was to write them – just as it is as much a bird's function to hatch its eggs as it was to lay them. It is for this reason, too, that he not only writes poetry but reads it – unless, as some do (and to my mind wrong-headedly), he consciously sets himself the task of disliking all poetry but his own. And it is for this reason also that the conscious study of technique is necessary to him – for technique is a slippery subject, and the Wild Men are all too ready to cry out against it, and call it a subject beneath the dignity of the artist: soul-fetters, tricks of the fake trade, and other hard names. But before embarking on that subject I have one more theory to broach.

It is a harder one to express clearly than the other two: and its corresponding definition is less self-obvious: but I would put it that Man is a Pattern-making Animal. From that follow two rather remote corollaries: first, that Art does not imitate Nature, but that Nature imitates Art: and secondly, that beauty is not predicable of Nature at all, but is a subjective mental process. For neither of the first two theories explains at all what is usually called beauty: they entirely ignore it; or else, assuming the old heresy that the useful is the beautiful, and having demonstrated poetry to be psycho-therapeutically useful, they so shelve rather than explain away the obvious phenomenon of its beauty. Moreover, neither of these theories explain adequately the phenomenon of rhythm; or, more important still, of that symbolism which plays such a large part both in the theories of psychoanalysis and in the corresponding theory of poetry (for even Freud himself seems now to have abandoned the censor-hypothesis). Nor do I attempt to explain them: only if I may be allowed to assume that the pattern-making instinct, which is common to all men and shared by no brutes – for such a device as the hexagonal shape of the cells in a honeycomb is not truly pattern-making, but rather a necessary mechanical expedient – if it is granted that this instinct is sufficiently fundamental to be used for purposes of definition, the rest naturally follows. Pattern is a crude form of rhythm, a skeleton of rhythm. Pattern itself is easiest described by the paradox that it is Identity with a Difference: and rhythm is pattern with a difference. What is logic itself but a kind of rhythmic thought, patterned conclusion? And it seems to me that it is not possible to divorce Beauty from some kind of rhythm or pattern. Why is it that a small child sees no beauty in a sunset, but screams with delight at a daisy? I would suggest that it is because he can see no pattern in a sunset, while a daisy does suggest a primitive sort of pattern to him. I lay emphasis on the word "suggest" because I would deny that you can call the daisy "beautiful". The process of visual beauty is that very process by which some visual impression evokes or suggests a pattern in the mind of the seer. But once that process has taken place in the mind of the artist, he creates an image, not truly of the object, but an image capable of suggesting more forcibly than the object itself could, a pattern in minds less sensitive than his. So the process of beauty is passed on: and so strong an impression does art make on the mind of the ordinary man, that the next time he sees actually the object which recently he had seen pictured; or an object similar to it; he is subconsciously reminded of the picture: the process of beauty is excited again; and his conscious mind, leaping the intermediate stages, calls the natural object "beautiful". This is what men mean when they state wrongly that the artist is an interpreter of nature.

But philosophy is a treacherous path for the imaginative man: and at any rate as far as poetry is concerned it is partly, though not wholly, irrelevant. I do not pretend to have put the position at all adequately, but to do so here at greater length would be disproportionate.

Poetry is the most abstract of the arts because it deals directly with thought – imagination – $\varepsilon\iota\delta\omega\lambda\alpha$ – idea – mental process – whatever it is that the mind does, makes. Thus, while plastic art deals entirely with those powers of imagination which correspond to the sense of sight, and music with those corresponding to the sense of hearing, poetry runs the gamut of all these senses, and comes back by way of a myriad of other mental activities that are not even sensory. Thus the technique of poetry is the technique of exciting, of setting in motion mental processes in another man's head; and thus far it is similar to the hypnotist's technique. By it the poet has to be able to excite vivid impressions of colour, of sound, of shape, smell, touch, taste: moreover, vivid conviction of the truth of more abstract things. But as I have suggested in the paragraph upon pattern-making, this is not in itself enough; or poetry could not be distinguished from poetical language, art from decoration. As well as vision there must be design: not merely a passable, mechanical design, but a *positive* excellence of construction, as well as astounding vision and phraseology: a design, moreover, in several dimensions: that is to say, there will be the sound – an orchestral effect – theme and counter-theme blended to an orchestral whole: the "counterpointing" of rhythm that Manley Hopkins studied with an assiduity almost too keen: this regulates the speed at which the successive words enter the reader's mind, and this is the real necessity for a vocal rhythm as a basis for mental rhythm. Then again, the orderly procession of ideas will also be guided by a rhythmic conception, whether those "ideas" be definite images, or images vague and inclusive, or purely non-sensory: and what is more, the conception of rhythm in all these dimensions will be influenced by their own interplay, as the painter does not follow one conception of colour, another of form, but a single welded concept – one picture.

These are but three of the many causes of poetry, chosen at random. To insist upon any one of them to the exclusion of all others, or even to insist upon all three thus exclusively must inevitably be productive of eccentricity in art: and eccentric theory is more likely to prove destructive to a man's expression than absence of all theory. But I think that the first is largely determined by the second and the third: that is to say, it is the instinct of communicativeness which incites the resolution of neuroses by verbal expression, and it is the instinct for pattern-making which determines the symbolical or poetical form of that expression.

The first problem to the poet, then, is vivid expression, and in this he has to remember that the reader is not his friend, but his enemy. The normal mind does not allow itself to be excited or to receive suggestions if it can help it. The poet has to outwit the reader and throw him off his guard. The attack must not come from the direction from which it is expected. To take an instance: if I were to turn suddenly to you and say "blue!", it conjures up in your mind only a faint impression of the colour; but if instead I said "Fields of cornflowers! Chests of sapphires! Italian skies!" in each case I think you will admit that the effect is far more vivid. This is a ridiculously simple example of the "Indirect Method". Your mind, quite ready to grapple with my attempts to force natural objects on you, was not prepared to withstand so simple a thing as a mere colour, and let that slip by. One might almost say that it is a rule only to mention the name of a colour under three circumstances: the first, when you wish to produce an impression of simplicity and naïveté – to pretend, as it were, that you didn't *know* the trick wouldn't come off, in order to have the reader off his guard for the next attack; the second, when the colour is not the usual colour of the object concerned; and third, when you quite consciously want to produce a dim effect. For instance in attempting a sea ballad, where it was essential that the general effect should be a highly-coloured one, the only colours I mentioned by name were that of the captain's skin, which was tanned red – a *dull* red, of course – and the green bilge, which too would be a dull green: all the vivid effects I attempted to produce indirectly.

This question of colour is a small one, but it serves as a useful example of this indirect method. In the same way, the poet capable of perceiving and ultimately establishing entirely new associations, excites as if it were by a Law of Reversed Action *immediate* repulsion in the reader, but the ultimate surrender is far more complete. Nothing is so abject as the mind finally converted to what it had detested.

One of the simplest forms of mental pattern is that produced by the relation of symbol to object: and in my opinion it is this that constitutes the tendency towards symbolism which is so characteristic of the human mind. Now the use of symbols, on its technical side, is also part of the indirect method. Consider God's sending of Nathan to David in 2 Samuel 12, verses 1-7. If Nathan had taxed David directly with his crime, what would have been the result? David would have probably sniffed and replied that the prophet's conception of morals was antiquated: that anyhow, Uriah was his subject, and if he chose to have him killed it was his loss alone: and that it was the sort of thing everybody did every day of their lives. Nathan, in fact, would entirely have failed to move the king. The poetical allegory itself, of course, is now so hackneyed a form that it has ceased to be effective: the poets of the Middle Ages have seen to that. The jaded reader is on the lookout for it: it is an old breech in his walls, and he posts double sentries there. But the allegory in its subtler form, the single metaphor, is still an effective weapon. Far more effective still is what I shall call the subconscious, as opposed to the conscious, use of symbolism. I refer to the subtle use of the associations of words, and to what Robert Graves used to call his Ghost theory of words. All words have these ghosts, and it is they that are very largely the material of poetry. When Aeneas wished to talk to his dead father Anchises, he dug a ditch and filled it with wine, honey, and goat's blood. Then swarms of ghosts crowded round and endeavoured to drink. But Aeneas pushed them back, all except those that he wished to hear speak: and that is what the poet has to do. Or rather, he cannot do anything so simple as to push them back: he cannot afford to let any single one of the assocations of a word pass right out of his mind: they have all to come into the pattern: and it is here that some of the infinite complexity of poetry comes in. It is like trying to build a wall of broken stones so that it should look like a Byzantine mosaic. Some words have such hopeless jags on them that they can never fit in anywhere: the cunning of the poet largely lies in his use of emphasis, by which he obliterates some ghosts that are going to spoil his pattern, and accentuates others. It is the associations, the stimulant action of words which form the poet's palette: and part of the necessary mental equipment of the "working poet" is an infinite delicacy of intoxication in words: I mean the delight, the very positive and ecstatic delight that a word or a phrase gives to him. It stimulates his faculty of beauty in the same way that a colour or line stimulates that of the painter. They acquire for him the depth of tone that is necessary if his construction is to have contrast. The wonder is, not that poetry is so difficult to write, but that it ever has been written at all. You may feel that it is the suggestion of this Preface that the writing of poetry is simply an exercise of conscious cleverness. On the contrary, I claim to have shown the impossibility of ever writing it that way: it is a task beyond human power. Earlier I likened it to the laying of an egg: I would press the analogy further: it is as impossible to construct a poem according to rules as it would be to construct a synthetic egg in a laboratory. You can analyse the egg afterwards, and you can analyse a poem: but the creation of either is a miracle performed by the internal organs.

What then of these rules, these "tricks of the trade" that I have attempted to formulate? There seems to me to be only one safe rule with regard to them: when writing journalism, use them to your heart's content: but when writing poetry, directly you are conscious of them, can formulate them, abandon them: otherwise they are simply putty in the cracks, and your poem will be a fake. The actual composition of poetry must be subconscious: your egg must be made in the stomach, not the laboratory. But to formulate them has this advantage, that it compels one to break new ground; and moreover, though one consciously abjures them, yet they find their way into the unconscious and still continue to play their unconscious part in one's work.

It may be objected that I have not once mentioned the word "metre", nor discussed the value of vowel-sounds, the more superficially musical aspects of verse. To this I plead guilty, but would tentatively suggest that neither is a subject of very great importance. Vocal rhythm regulates to a nicety the reader's speed: the exact moment at which each suggestion shall enter his mind: it is therefore essential that besides possessing a surface beauty of its own it should closely correspond to the image-pattern, the rhythm of associations: but if the latter is delicately felt, surely it will itself be sufficient to inspire the former – if the poet has any ear at all. If the mental pattern is to be original – which is of course essential – the vocal rhythm must be original too. It sets the time for the rest: that is its chief function: without it the mental rhythm is liable to collapse. That is why successful *vers libre* is so difficult to write: if it is rhythmic, rhythm which does not consist in variation from metre is so much more easily misinterpreted by the reader (who acts as a kind of executioner), while if it is not rhythmic, it will depend almost entirely for its effect on being read in such bulk that irregularities in the reader's speed become negligible.

This Preface began with an apology for its existence: and it shall end with one. Whether the critic dub it heretical or platitudinous, it is my hope that he may at least find it explanatory of some of the less accountable of my vagaries.

1921

Illogic and the Child

A certain author took a parcel of children's stories to his publisher. The latter read them, and gave his verdict:

"There seems to me only one thing wrong with these children's stories of yours," he said: "Namely, that they are written for children."

The author kept his face a polite, enquiring blank.

"We can't publish them. The only children's stories that we or anybody else can publish are those written for adults. I should have thought you would have realized that for yourself."

"I had realized," said the author, "that the majority of so-called stories for children were plainly aimed far more at the parent: but in my innocence I had considered this a defect that I hoped to remedy."

"And who do you think *buys* children's books?" continued the exasperated publisher: "Do you think the children read the reviews? Do you think the children go to the store and browse about till they find something which takes their fancy? No, a book for children must appeal to adults, first, last, and all the time."

With which, the unfortunate author was put out on his ear.

* * *

This little tale is not wholly imaginary: the state of affairs which it depicts is not imaginary at all. That it is the parents' approval which constitutes financial success or failure, nobody is likely to question. And one has only to look at a shelfful of examples to convince oneself that the average children's book is written as much, if not more, for the parents.

But it is much too early in my argument, yet, to say offhand that these hermaphrodites are to be condemned. After all, Shakespeare, that greatest exponent of the club-sandwich in literature, wrote so as to please both the groundlings and the intellectuals. Whoever bit found something to his taste. So why should not an author be able in the same

work, sandwich-wise, to please both child and parent? Theoretically it
should be possible. And there are in existence a few classics, such as
Alice in Wonderland, which prove that it is possible, even in practice.

But they are very, very few. It is their scarcity which is the most
eloquent witness to the almost unparalleled difficulty of the task.

This difficulty, to my mind, springs from a fundamental difference of
kind between writing for children, and writing for adults: a difference
far greater than that between writing for the groundlings and writing
for the intellectuals: a difference so wide that it can never be bridged –
one can only build on both sides of the gap at once, so that at least to the
distant or casual observer the edifice shall appear to be a single,
undivided whole.

For the moment let us take it for granted that we know what we mean
by writing for adults, and that we are in happy agreement on all points
concerning it. We can then concern ourselves entirely with that more
alien architecture on the far side of the gap, with writing for children
only.

But allow me a parenthesis first. On almost any subject one is prone
to generalize too readily and too casually: but one is especially ready to
say children this, and children that, as if ''children'' was a definite
natural term like manganese dioxide. One forgets, in the excitement of
argument, if not the truism itself, at least the truth of the truism that
they are a parcel of individuals as unlike one another as adults. They
may be as unlike as Julius Caesar and Bottom the Weaver. It is highly
dangerous to use the phenomena of a single example as the basis of a
general law. It is as rash to affirm that, because one child (your own,
perhaps,) likes this or that, ''children'' do, as to affirm that because
your iceman reads the tabloids so do all Democrats.

But the pitfalls of all generalization are even more cunningly hidden
than that. The term ''childhood'' itself we use with an unholy
looseness, to cover every age from babyhood to full adolescence, as if we
supposed that every human life was neatly divided into two halves.
Whereas it would be far truer to represent childhood itself as a series of
successive periods so dissimilar that the changes from one to another
are at least as drastic as those of adolescence (which is only the last of
them): periods which have little in common except their unfamiliarity
to the adult, their uniform opacity to the mature eye.

So, if I appear to make any definite statement about ''children'', I
make it, be it understood, with the utmost diffidence. So far from
claiming it to be true of all children, I hardly even claim it to be true of

most children – I only suspect it to be. Further, by "childhood" I mean a fairly limited stage, which it is difficult to confine to any particular age but which is generally at its most characteristic between five and eight.

At any rate, this is the age to which the majority of books for children purport to be addressed.

Now, the strange thing about this stage of mental development – strange to the adult human eye, at least, though perhaps not so strange to the eye of God – is its very democratic attitude towards Reason.

We all know, of course, that the logical system is only one of a great many possible systems of thought-association. But the Aristotelian hegemony of the last twenty-five hundred years has taught us to suppress and vilify all others, to deny them any validity. It is only with the advent of psycho-analysis that they have at least come in for serious consideration. But even psycho-analysis, though it may use illogical thought for its material, draws its conclusions from that material in a logical manner – as any science, in the present state of the meaning of the word science, is bound to do. Psycho-analysis, though recognizing for the first time their empirical importance, and the enormous extent of the dissident thinking which they govern, has done nothing yet to question the ultimate sovereignty of logic. It still retains its absolute validity, it still remains the system to which all other systems must finally be referred.

The new physics tells us that all possible "frames of space", though contradictory, are equally valid – that any search for a frame of ultimate, sovereign validity is not only impossible but also downright nonsense. The substitution of "systems of thought-association" for "frames of space" in this statement will give us, I think, a picture not too far-fetched to be of value in understanding one at least of the essential differences between the childish and the adult mind. For the latter, while recognizing the existence of other systems, looks upon one of them – logic – as having an especial, sovereign validity. But to the child, reason has no such peculiar validity, is hedged by no divinity. At most it is *primus inter pares:* and frequently its position is a humbler one even than that.

Now art is (to use a mathematical idiom) a function of mentality. It is perfectly true that a piece of literature even for adults which employed no system of thought-connection in its texture other than the purely logical would hardly deserve the name of literature at all. But it is equally true (except in the case of pure ecstatic poetry) that it is bound to take logic for the backbone, to relate all other systems to it. Especially is this true in the case of fiction: the skeleton, the main progression must be acceptable to reason (which, of course, is not at all the same thing as saying it must necessarily be probable in nature) whatever the super-structure. But in writing for children, this is not necessary – not even desirable!

What logical connection of thought enters into a story for children enters there only on equal terms. It certainly has no patent to give itself airs.

*   *   *

What books did you like as a child? How difficult it is to remember . . . at least, it is difficult to remember with absolute honesty. But try to compile a list: and then compare it with what your friends liked in their time – friends of your own age, friends of an older generation, and also those children that you are in contact with now.

There will be a few classics that will crop up in almost every list, perhaps: but hardly any that you will not find someone anxious to blackball, sooner or later – why, there are even plenty of children, otherwise normal little protanthropies, who detest *Alice in Wonderland.* Probably almost the only noticeable feature of any such collection of lists will be their unlimited variety. Dickens, mythology, Scott, popular science, purple passion, Hans Andersen, satire, nature study, adventure, Kipling, and sheer unadulterated uplift – all may be expected to find their places. And poetry. I know one little girl who detested reading of every kind until one day she happened to overhear a grown-up reading aloud a poem of Edith Sitwell's. ''Read that again!'' she demanded, for the first time in her life: and presently command-eered the book by force.

In short, such lists will be almost as varied as would be similar lists of the likes of adults. To consider them all would require the windy length of an encyclopaedia, rather than the constriction of a periodical-article. And so, if I confine myself to the class which seems to me in some ways the most characteristic – namely, illogical fiction – it is not through bigotry, Gentle Reader.

*   *   *

It may be objected that if the mind of the adult is essentially logical, how can it possibly produce fiction that is truly illogical: fiction for children can only be written by children: and indeed, there is something in the objection. In a normal state it is, if not impossible, at least very difficult. And yet we all of us compose illogical fiction, reams of it, in our sleep. But that we do for our own purposes, not to order. The insistent "Tell us a story!" has proved the knell of many an otherwise fertile imagination. The power may be there, but it is dormant: it lacks the impulse.

But it is possible. Especially if one lives for a time in close companionship with children towards whom one is in no kind of a position of responsibility, even the bigoted adult mind slips surprisingly quickly into habits of purely associative thinking. Then, all that one needs to be able to tell stories as readily as dreaming is a slight initial impulse. My own recipe for that initial impulse is a simple one, but I have never known it to fail – and I suppose I must have told upwards of a thousand such stories, at one time or another. Ask each child in your audience for one, or perhaps two, ingredients for the story. One chooses an elephant, let us say, and one an aeroplane and one a lobster-trap and one a man with a luminous green face and one a prime minister. Immediately the imagination is off, starting from one, spinning its web to the next, and so on to the next and back again – one can hardly tell it fast enough. Of course, it is rather like tight-rope walking: one may easily be upset *en route*. For me, the presence of an adult in my audience is often enough to set me floundering hopelessly. And as might be expected, one seldom remembers afterwards much of what one has said. It passes, like the waves of the sea that leave no mark on the wind which produced them.

Yet even the waves of the sea mark the shore: and what the teller forgets the audience often remembers with an almost verbal fidelity. I cannot "write" children's stories, I can only tell them in the way I have described. Such stories for children as I have published (mostly in English magazines) have been retold to me, sometimes as late as six months afterwards, by the children to whom they were told, and so taken down. Sometimes, when they were retold to me in this way, I recalled them: at other times they were as strange as if I had never heard them before. But I generally found, where it was possible to check up by having them told to me by two of the audience separately, that the form in which they came back to me must have been almost word for word the form in which they were first told.

I hasten to add that I do not necessarily claim any great merit for these stories of mine, other than what was inherent in their nature. Many of them were undoubtedly, even as illogic, sheer piffle, which might hold the audience at the time but were not remembered by them afterwards and did not deserve to be. At the same time, it would be highly interesting to know how the great masterpieces of illogical fiction came to be written. How came the story of the ''Three Bears'', which is imbedded in the amiable but surely not immortal bulk of *The Doctor,* somewhat as the story of ''Cupid and Psyche'' is embedded in *The Golden Asse,* into the mind of Laureate Southey? How did the White Rabbit first come to hurry across the imagination of that painstaking mathematician, the Rev. C.L. Dodgson? Had ''Alice'' herself perhaps some part in its genesis? Or must one look for it entirely in the imagery of the author's own subconscious?

There is another problem too, in connection with *Alice,* that is no less interesting, and more possible of investigation. How comes it that of all the works of illogical fiction this particular one should receive the almost universal approbation of adults? It is easy to discount it, of course, by pointing to the hidden satire, the parodies of well-known poems, and so on: to regard it as a supreme example of the sandwich. But there is more in it than that. *Alice* seems actually to appeal to adults *in the same way* that it appeals to children. There is a power, a vividness in its imagery that is not shared by its weaker brethren: so powerful, that it can upset for a time the very throne of logic itself, can turn the mind of an adult for the time being into the mind of a child. Just in what this superior force lies it is hard to say: but that it works in this way, there can be little doubt.

I was recently at the sick bed of a friend, a man in his forties, an eminent and enthusiastic architect who practically never read a book and certainly had no unusual liking for children. He was very ill, and most of the time delirious. In his delirium he was pestered by a horde of clients, demanding plaques, belvederes, heating-plants – but chiefly plaques. We tried every obvious means of routing them: notices

NO PLAQUES REQUIRED

and so on, were posted all over the room. For a time they worked: but the moment he took his eyes off them, back came the insistent horde. Then someone thought of reading him *Alice* and we read it for hours and hours. It worked. The imagery was so powerful, that although coming from without it was able to banish the imagery of his own delirium.

It is a far cry from a work like this, which can capture the adult by the sheer strength of its childishness to the sandwich proper, to the story which is continually gesticulating to the parent behind the child's back. I repeat that I mean no disrespect to these latter: a typical example of which is the "Christopher Robin" series, a more delicate one the lovely stories of Margery Williams Bianco. It is a churlish criticism, that the story pleases too many. But all the same I cannot help wishing that there were a larger body of literature for children only – the reservation being not due to any lack of merit, but only to its specialization.

Saturday Review of Literature
15th November, 1930

The Birth of Radio Drama

The Birth of Radio Drama, as a title, suggests a solemn, formal occasion. But things were very casual in the early days of "listening in to the wireless", and this historic birthday – January 15, 1924 – was no exception.

In those days the program department of the BBC was virtually a one-man affair, and the director of programs himself filled in time as "Uncle Caractacus" in the children's hour. I can't recall the date I first "spoke on the wireless" myself but I think it was during the winter of 1922-1923; at any rate I had never even seen a radio receiving set at the time and only half believed in them. I was shown into a large empty room like something in Sartre and told to talk to nobody at all, and I found it hard to believe the whole thing was not a huge practical joke on me.

Regular entertainment broadcasting was first rendered possible by wartime developments in radio-telephony between 1914 and 1918. But until 1922 it was still at the experimental stage – homemade crystal sets, and listeners too excited by hearing anything at all to care what they heard. It was not till early in 1922 that the first regular scheduled programs began to be broadcast in Britain for half an hour a week. The first broadcast concert came in July that year; in August the first London station, 2LO, was established on the roof of Marconi House; and in November the "British Broadcasting Company" came into official being as a program-transmitting monopoly.

During the next twelve months broadcasting developed rapidly – in Britain, on the Continent, and in the U.S.A. – especially on the musical side. The BBC's very successful transmission in January, 1923, of Mozart's *Magic Flute* from the Covent Garden Opera House was a landmark. Other operas followed: it was natural that music should take the lead, for its performance required little or no adaptation to the new medium, and in the case of opera many music lovers found it an actual advantage not to have to see their voluminous divas as well as hear them. But the spoken word, in those days, was still confined to the news bulletin and the cozy "talk". It was some time before it occurred to anyone that here was an opportunity for a new literary form altogether – something deriving from the stage play but differing from it as widely as the silent film did. When that time came, it came more or less by accident.

I don't mean that early program authorities were blind to the possibility of dramatic performances other than opera being broadcast; only that they did not at first think beyond adaptation – a mere sort of keyhole listening, eavesdropping, at the theater. Indeed in the winter of 1922-1923 the BBC invited Nigel Playfair to undertake a dramatic entertainment of just this kind. Nigel Playfair was at that time perhaps the most famous theatrical director in London; he had built up the Lyric Theatre, Hammersmith, out of nothing, and his revolutionary production of *The Beggar's Opera* had just ended a four-year run there. An innovator, but steeped in the classical tradition, with a flair for popularity: surely just the man to make a successful three-point landing on such an occasion.

It was to take place on January 15, 1924. Playfair began to make up his bill. He decided on some of Vachel Lindsay's chanted poetry; one of A.P. Herbert's humorous dialogues, read in parts; the proposal scene from *Pride and Prejudice,* also read in parts. The program was to last two hours and a fourth item was needed.

That fourth item was still to be found on Friday, January 11, four days before the broadcast was to take place. It so happened that I was dining with Playfair that night. Hospitably he had offered his theater for a brief London appearance to a small company of Welsh players I was interested in (I was twenty-three at the time, and this was my first and last experience as an actor-manager). So we met to discuss the forthcoming visit, but somehow soon got to talking about this new business of broadcasting, and he told me his program for Tuesday was still undecided. "Broadcasting is a new kind of entertainment altogether," he said. "Really what it wants is new stuff – stuff specially written for it."

I had come to that conclusion myself already and inwardly wished I had had this chance.

As if Playfair read my thoughts, he cocked his eye at me and said, "Pity I didn't think of it in time to get you to write something! But I've promised to give them the final program tomorrow. Casts to engage and so on."

But was it too late, after all? In those days my mind was a ferment of themes for plays, and I was fired with the possibilities of the radio form. The loss of a night's sleep wouldn't worry me. Without hesitation I undertook to write a new play to be delivered next day at Playfair's breakfast table.

That settled, we talked around the project for a while. Sounds – how they are even more distinctive than sights: a teaspoon on a saucer, kicking a football, tearing paper, opening a bottle – the ear recognizes them instantly without any help from the eye. Moreover, what a much less jaded organ emotionally the ear is than the eye!

There would be special difficulties. *Seemingly* we were attempting no more, in essaying to stir the emotions and tell a complete story through a single organ, the ear, than what the cinema already did through the eye. But in practice no film – even the silent film of those days – relied on visual pictures alone; for subtitles are really disguised sound. Moreover, movie houses in those days generally kept a sad musician thumping themes emotionally appropriate on a piano throughout the performance. Some of the grander ones even employed an "effects man" who wound a wind machine in the storm scenes and accompanied the galloping cowboy with clashing coconut shells. We could have no auxiliary recourse to a second sense, no equivalent of subtitles – for we agreed that to use a narrator would be a confession of failure. Our "listening play" must rely on dramatic speech and sound entirely.

It had never been done before; that was the especial rub, for it meant we had a totally inexperienced audience to deal with. We were plunging them into a blind man's world. No doubt in time they would get used to it and come to accept its conventions, but how would they react this first time they were suddenly struck blind? We agreed that, this once at any rate, something must be done to make it easier for them. A story for example which really happens in the dark, so that the characters themselves keep complaining they can't see. Then perhaps the announcer could ask the audience to put out their lights and listen in darkness, too, so as to feel themselves in the very middle of the action they were hearing.

"Here's a first speech for you," said Playfair as he escorted me to the door: *"The lights have gone out!"*

Back in my attic flat in New Oxford Street I turned over possible situations in my mind. *The lights have gone out!* Not a bedroom scene. To be candid, I did not know much about bedrooms, even at twenty-three.

An accident in a coal mine? I knew nothing about coal mines either, and there was no time to find out. But technically the theme seemed to offer the sort of things I wanted: sudden total darkness, the dramatic sounds of explosions and rushing water, the picks of a rescue team. But wouldn't miners' voices, if the characters were all miners, be too difficult to tell apart? A party of visitors, then, lost in the mine? An old man, a young man, a girl?

I wrote all night and delivered the play (which I called *A Comedy of Danger*) as I had promised.

A few hours later it was in rehearsal, and our real troubles began. Rashly, I had made great play in my script with sound effects, without seriously considering how these were to be produced. It was all very well to talk glibly at the dinner table about sounds, but producing them convincingly in the studio was a different kettle of fish. Someone ran round the corner and enlisted the "effects man" from a cinema in the Strand, wind machine and all, but still we could make nothing sound as it was meant to sound even in the studio. We had not taken into account the primitive transmission of those days that, as we soon discovered, reduced all sounds – tinkle of teaspoon, clash of swords, footsteps, the roar of Niagara – to a single indistinguishable *wump*.

Not even the voices sounded right. The studio of those days was a vast padded cell designed to make all voices sound as if they were floating in outer space; how were we to make these sound like people cramped together in an underground flooded tunnel? There was as yet no artificial echo to be had by twiddling a knob. So Playfair decreed that his whole cast must orate with their handsome heads in buckets.

The script called for occasional "distant snatches of hymn singing" from entombed Welsh miners. In those days unemployed Welsh miners were singing in the London streets for coppers; it was easy enough to engage a choir. They sang beautifully and with passion, but once started nothing could stop them. How could their performance be reduced to "snatches", with only one studio and one microphone? Playfair stationed them to sing in the corridor, outside a soundproof door he could open and shut at will.

The climax came when we told the engineers we wanted an explosion. They answered that if we so much as popped a paper bag near the microphone it would blow every fuse in Savoy Hill. In my innocence I had counted on a terrific roar and rumble of falling rock that would batter on the ears, but Shakespeare's roaring of a sucking dove would be a deafening sound compared with all the "explosion" they were prepared to allow us.

The press was treating this as an important occasion. Reporters and critics were to assemble and listen in the building, in a room specially equipped for them. On their verdict, we felt, the whole future of this infant art might depend. Even if the public must hear only a diminutive *wump,* the press (Playfair decreed) must hear something better. So he secretly arranged for a magnificient, catastrophic explosion in the room next door to them. They thought it came to them with the rest of the play through the loudspeaker; in fact they heard it through the wall.

Thus, then, did radio drama emit its first faint infant wail.

A few months later, finding myself in New York, I tried to interest American radio authorities in the newborn child. Their response is curious when you consider how very popular radio plays were later to become in the States. They stood me good luncheons; they listened politely; but then they rejected the whole idea. That sort of thing might be possible in England, they explained, where broadcasting was a monopoly and a few crackpot highbrows in the racket could impose what they liked on a suffering public. But the American setup was different: it was competitive, so it had to be popular, and it stood to reason that plays you couldn't see could never be popular. Yet it was not very long before these specially written ''blind'' plays (my own *Comedy of Danger* among them) began to be heard in America, and on the European continent as well. *A Comedy of Danger* moreover soon began to find a use for which it had never been intended: it was obviously impossible to give it in a theater, but it became surprisingly popular with amateur companies on both sides of the Atlantic. For it was a godsend for them at last to find a play which needed no scenery, no costumes; all you had to do for a setting was put out the lights. It did not even need a stage: in total darkness it could be acted in any living room.

I have gone on to this day writing radio scripts of all kinds, though only occasionally and never (I must confess) quite wholeheartedly. Deterrents have been at work, but not things inherent in the medium, only accidental, remediable things. They can all be summed up in one word: time.

Radio drama needs more time than it has ever been allotted if it is to grow to its potential stature. More time, first, for writing: harbingers, perhaps, but not masterpieces can be written in a single night. I know of only one radio play which does approach classic level; the gestation of *Under Milk Wood* took thirteen years, from that night in 1939 when it was first conceived. Time in this case means money: money to live on.

More time is needed, too, for production. No theatrical producer would dare to put a production on the boards in the state most productions go on the air; his cast would still be reading their parts round a table. It takes weeks of work, not days, to extract the full savor of serious dramatic writing. How can a writer be expected to write in depth when he knows that producer and cast will have no time to do more than skim his surface?

What are the remedies, then, considering that the resources both of time and money are limited? There need be no further call on those resources if only radio plays were performed *more often*, as stage plays are performed and books printed, so that what is great has time to be sifted from the ephemeral. There should be a regular policy of repetition and revival, so that the better plays have a chance to rise to the top. Fewer new plays and more repetition of old ones would mean more adequate rewards for the efforts of those writers whose plays deserve repetition, more time for the producer to do his work properly, and more incentive too.

Sound radio has shown sufficient vigor to survive its first crisis, the coming of television. But if there is now to be any development in sound radio comparable with the development of the Elizabethan theater, then I think the program authorities themselves will have to play their part. There is much for them to ponder; there are new policies to be formed: *they* will have to begin to take radio drama seriously. Only then can we hope that someday the true birthday of radio drama will be dated not January 15, 1924 – the night of the first broadcast of *A Comedy of Danger* – but a night thirty years later: January 25, 1954, the first broadcast of *Under Milk Wood*.

The Atlantic Monthly
December, 1957

Introduction to *A High Wind in Jamaica*

Some 40 years ago, when I was a young man just down from Oxford, a friend of the family happened to show me – just as a matter of passing interest – a few sheets of paper she kept in the bottom of a drawer. The pencil-writing on them was faint and tremulous and spidery, but the letters were elegantly formed; it was the hand of a very old lady, of Queen Victoria's own generation. It recorded an incident from the writer's own childhood, and the incident was a singular one.

In the year 1822 (she wrote) she was one of a party of children from Jamaica being shipped home to England in the brig 'Zephyr' when the brig was captured by pirates just off the coast of Cuba. Apparently 'Zephyr' carried quite a large sum *in specie* hidden aboard, and somehow the pirates knew it. (Was Aaron Smith, the mysterious new mate, she afterwards wondered, in league with them? Had he tipped them off?) But Lumsden, master of the 'Zephyr', obdurately denied that he carried any money at all: and though they ransacked her from stem to stern, they could not find it. To make Lumsden talk, they then told him he should see all the children in his charge murdered before his eyes if he would not give up the money. But the money, after all, was his own and the children weren't, a point the pirates had overlooked: even when a preliminary volley aimed just over the children's heads was fired into the deckhouse where they were huddled, Lumsden remained quite unmoved. On that the pirates let the children out of the deckhouse and rowed them over to their own schooner, considerately wanting them out of sight and earshot while more direct (and ultimately more successful) means of persuasion were applied to Lumsden's own tender person. Over there in the pirate schooner, moreover, the children found themselves petted and made much of, and feasted on crystallized fruit. Indeed, they were given such a whale of a party by the pirates they were quite tearful when the time came to say goodbye to their new friends and be put back in the brig again.

Here the brief penciled story ended. Lumsden by now had given in, the pirates had their money as well as other loot, and the two vessels parted. It was Aaron Smith the pirates finally carried off with them and not the children.

But . . . suppose through some accident the children had *not* been returned to the brig and the loving care of Captain Lumsden at all? Suppose these all-too-human pirates had found themselves saddled indefinitely with the whole lethal nursery-load of them . . .

A very young man (which is all I was when the theme of *A High Wind in Jamaica* tumbled into my lap like this) is seldom really ripe for novel-writing: he is still more of an age for writing shorter things at a burst. On all counts it seemed better to put off beginning the book till I should be at least twenty-five or -six; and in the meantime I decided to pitch my story a whole generation later than the 'Zephyr' incident – in the decadence of old-time piracy rather than its heyday, when the really tough guys had mostly drifted away to new and more profitable rackets. For Aaron Smith, as I presently discovered, had survived to stand his trial ("looking very gentlemanly in a black suit") and, after his acquittal, to write his memoirs. (*The Atrocities of the Pirates* by Aaron Smith was first published in 1824. Entirely by coincidence, it was reprinted at the Golden Cockerel Press in 1929, the same year that *A High Wind in Jamaica* first appeared.) The generation of pirates Smith described was altogether too conventionally beastly for a book like mine.

When the time did come for an actual beginning, I retired to the exquisite little Adriatic island-town of Capodistria, where the exchange was then so favourable I could live on next to nothing – which was all I had – and where the only language spoken was Italian, of which (at first at any rate) I knew not a word, so that I could work all day in the Café della Loggia undisturbed by the chatter: to me it was just meaningless sound, no more interruptious than wind or rain. There for a whole winter I wrestled with the first chapter. This may seem slow going: but I had decided my book was to be a short one and it is always what a writer leaves out of his book which takes the time, not what he puts in. When at last – driven out by my increasing understanding of Italian – I got back to Britain, I offered this first chapter to Henry Goddard Leach in New York and he printed it in the *Forum* as a separate short story. This chapter was the hurricane one: "I liked your high wind in Jamaica," he wrote; and I in my turn liked his phrase, adopting it forthwith as title of the whole book-to-come.

Presently I followed this first chapter across the Atlantic myself, with my now half-finished manuscript as my principal luggage, on a visit to old friends – a happy visit that was somehow prolonged for 18 months. So it was there in America that I finished the book at last, living alone by that time (on a budget of $10 a week) in an old frame house near New Preston, Connecticut. That is how it happened that the book appeared in New York some months before it appeared in London, and the *first* edition is really the American one. (It appeared, alas, under a changed title, *The Innocent Voyage;* but the rest of the world knew it from the first under the original one, and later American editions have been known some by one name, some by the other.)

On its first appearance, certain New York reviewers fought for it in season and out of season; but readers were slow to respond. At that moment everybody was reading Joan Lowell's *Cradle of the Deep,* and the public could hardly be expected to swallow two child-at-sea books at once. In its original edition *The Innocent Voyage* came nowhere near the sacred circle of bestsellerdom. In spite of this slow start, however, in the more-than-30 years which have since elapsed, it has never once been out of print in America, and the reprint editions have tended to grow progressively larger. Moreover, it was an American not long ago who threw discretion to the winds and called it "the best novel about children ever written" – a thing no European has ever said for quotation.

On the other hand, in London and in Europe generally, wide and instant success seemed to fall on it out of the blue the moment it appeared, chiefly, I think, because it gave people something to argue about. For not everybody liked it, of course; there were child-lovers who came to the boil and boiled over about it. André Gide didn't like it: he could see no reason why it had ever been written. The headmistress of the Royal School for Officers' Daughters at Bath didn't like it either; she was sure none of *her* little charges would ever murder a grownup, but if they did they were truthful children and could be relied on (like George Washington) to own up – she wrote to the papers to say so.

Someone said recently that this book "in its quiet way" has done more to change people's ideas about childhood than all the works of Freud: but I myself was entirely astonished at the controversy my innocent tale aroused. I had not set out to change anybody's ideas about anything. I had a story to tell. My story chanced to be about children . . . but surely children had the same right their elders had to be portrayed as realistically as I knew how. After all, in such a context, "realistically" is only another word for "lovingly"; my whole concern was to show them at their truthfullest best – with love.

But if I am now asked what this book means to me today, I can say absolutely nothing except that I know there was once a time when it fitted me like a glove. I went on growing, however; I had to shed it (to write it, that is to say). There it now lies before you – part of me no longer; and how can a writer's attitude to his own past work ever be other than the strictly "no comment" one of the growing snake toward the skin he has sloughed?

1963

Fear and *In Hazard*

How unlucky the man would be, who was born without fear!

Unlucky, because he would not live long. He would succumb to the first danger he met.

The instinct of fear is not only valuable, it is invaluable. It is essential to the maintenance of life: like pain.

Pain warns you that there is something wrong with your body, and urges you to remedy it quickly. Fall in the fire, and pain urges you to get out again quickly. If you felt no pain, you might quite possibly stop there till you were dead.

But pain is a warning that does not always come soon enough. By the time pain is felt, some at least of the damage is done: it may be too late to escape (if you waited till you felt the pain of being run over by a bus, for instance, it would probably be too late to escape).

An earlier warning is needed; and that warning is given by fear. It is a warning moreover which generally comes in time, because as a rule it comes before any physical damage has been done.

It is difficult to realise what an important and valuable part in our lives is played by fear. We are so used to treating it as a bogey – something to be ashamed of and fought against, the source of every mean and wicked thing we do – that we forget the good it does. Actually, the answer to nearly every problem of conduct we ordinarily set ourselves is given by fear. The *right* answer, I mean. Where we have the choice of two things to do, we do the wise thing because we are afraid of the consequences of doing the foolish thing.

But fear, like so many of the would-be automatic devices of nature, does not always in practice serve the purposes it is intended to serve. It does not always tend to preserve us.

Compare it with hunger and thirst. Hunger and thirst are also intended to keep us alive, by making us want to eat and drink. But what happens if the hungry man is offered poisoned food, or the thirsty man is offered sea-water? Hunger and thirst will urge them on just the same:

will urge them to do something actually dangerous to life. Then, to be saved, you must resist those natural urges.

It is the same with fear. Fear too is blind. Reason may show you the only possible escape from a dangerous position: but if that path itself is dangerous, fear will try to prevent you taking it. If you persist, you will feel fear pulling you back, you will feel your strength running out of the heels of your boots and your wits getting as addled as an old egg.

That paralysis is one of the effects of fear: and a very dangerous one it is.

A common form of it is the fear of heights. You may easily be incapable of walking along a nine-inch girder a hundred feet above a street – equally unable to do it, whether or not you are escaping from a house on fire: but you could walk along a nine-inch strip painted on the pavement with no difficulty at all. That is the sort of fear which must be most rigorously controlled, because in an emergency it may be exceedingly dangerous; if not to yourself, at least to others.

Yet that is by no means the only way in which fear can affect you. With some people – a few – it seems to act in the reverse way. It acts as a tonic, it makes them more efficient, not less. I will tell you an astonishing story of that. A child had just learnt to bicycle, and was annoyed with herself because she could not ride straight along the garden path without tumbling into the flowerbeds. So she took her machine down to the big, main-road bridge over the river, and bicycled along the top of the stone parapet: and the fear of falling to her death actually kept her straight!

I am writing this to try and explain, as well as I can, part of the purpose which caused me to write *In Hazard*. It is a book about fear.

Perhaps one of the worst misfortunes which can befall a book is a sudden wide success: because that success is often due to something more or less irrelevant which comes to cause the main theme of the book to escape notice. This happened with my first book, *A High Wind in Jamaica:* and it seems to have happened again with *In Hazard*. For, so far as I can judge, the latter has been successful because the description of the storm is said to be vivid and the story to be exciting. That has made people say that the book is "about" a storm, and that the men in it hardly matter (I suppose if the description of a storm is vivid enough to make you feel that *you* are in it, you are liable to forget about your fellow-sufferers, the characters in the book!) – but I don't believe that a thoughtful reader would agree altogether with that verdict. He would notice that in the shipload of men exposed to that appalling and prolonged danger almost every possible effect of fear, good and bad, has its expression. In Mr. Rabb and the Chinese crew you see the paralysing effect of panic. In the captain you see the opposite, the way fear can stimulate a man to do things beyond his ordinary powers. In the mate, Mr. Buxton, you see the disciplined reaction of a man who can so control fear that it does not effect his efficiency either way. In the others – in the elderly chief engineer and most of all in the junior officer Dick Watchett – you see (what would probably be your own case in an emergency) the interplay of all these different effects, now one now another holding sway. And you see the effect on fear of the imagination, and the effect on the imagination of conquering fear.

In Dick's case, too, you see the effect of that curious incident with the young girl Sukie; and the reaction which inuring himself to danger has on his love for her. For you can have no experience by which you gain without paying for it. Just as a boy, when his singing voice breaks and he gets his new bass notes, loses for ever the treble ones, so you *cannot* acquire the power of enduring, with sangfroid, continual danger of death without losing, at the other end of the scale, your finer sensitiveness.

If I had emphasised this theme, exaggerated the psychology of fear a little, dotted all my I's and crossed my T's, the book would have been morbid – and false. But because I gave the theme no more weight than what is natural, some readers, it seems, have never noticed what the book is about!

1938

Introduction to *In Hazard*

When this novel was first published, the line taken in a brief prefatory note was this: "The events in this story have been kept . . . strictly within the bounds of scientific possibility: the bounds of what has happened, or can happen . . . ."

That note, which is also found in this edition, was written a long time ago. There were good reasons then for this mere half-truth; but today there can be none for not being more explicit. This *is* a novel, a story about people who never existed; *but the whole inanimate side of it is fact.*

Once, in recent meteorological history, there really had been a hurricane as stupendous and as unpredicted as the one here recorded, and a British cargo steamer very like the 'Achimedes' did live through it – just. Day by day, hour by hour, minute by minute that storm did behave in detail as is here narrated.

But there fact ends. For purposes of my novel I signed on a new and wholly imaginary crew. There are no *human* portraits here, for this would neither have been decent behaviour to the men themselves nor would it have served my purposes as a novelist.

I examined that steamer from stem to stern while a crusted water line (from the 1,000 tons of sea she had shipped), slanting diagonally up the bulkheads dividing her holds, was still there to prove the incredible angle of the list she had taken and how near she had been to filling; while one could still see and handle cold steel torn and twisted like paper, tangled like string. I studied her logs and track charts. I questioned deck officers and engineers while their experience was still liquid in them so that, however reticent their normal natures, for the time being they could not help but talk and talk and talk. A little later, and in another command, I went to sea with her master. Thus I was able to piece together their several stories until possessed of the complete narrative of everything which had happened, in the material sense, in every several part of her: until I knew more about the total effects of that wind than any one of them separately knew.

How did I get this rare chance? The answer is simple: her owners felt that an event so extraordinary must never be forgotten. They had sent for me, as for some kind of tribal bard.

But why did I jump at the chance when I got it?

Here the answer is much less simple. I was already in the throes of another novel which this new project would have to elbow into limbo. The book moreover would be utterly unlike anything else I had written or expected to write – or, indeed, was fitted by experience to write, for I had never been to sea in steam (any more than, before writing *A High Wind in Jamaica ,* I had ever been a little girl). The work involved would be immense. Why, then, this interest in an alien and merely true event so compulsive that I felt under the Muse's explicit orders to drop everything else and write it?

At the time of writing I was only aware of the compulsion: I had no glimmer of a notion *why.* Now, looking back, I do think I begin to see at least one reason. But to explore it calls for some rather recondite delving into the general motivation of imaginative writing; and perhaps at this point even the thoughtful reader (the other sort skips introductions anyway) would rather turn on to the story itself.

He will find a plain sea story about men in a storm (it is quite short and, although it took four years to write, can be read at a sitting). He can then come back, if he still wants to, abler to judge whether what follows here has a likely ring; but unless he has a real lust for taking the lids off writers to see how the wheels go round he had better not come back at all, for he may find what follows a rather rarefied and theoretical introduction to any plain sea story about men in a storm!

My own inclination in any such inquiry is to start from the premise of those who hold (the young Robert Graves was among the first to suggest it) that the writing of poetry does for the poet what dreaming does for Tom, Dick and Harry: it allows a safe outlet for conflicts and tensions too painful for his conscious mind to face, disguised so impenetrably in symbol that the poet himself has no inkling of what his poem is really "about" – just as the dreamer has none till his analyst tells him. The tension both determines the symbol and generates the compulsive force. Moreover, let me stress from the start the fundamental difference between symbol (in this dream sense) and conscious allegory: the poet's absolute ignorance of what he is really saying seems to be necessary if the magic is to work. A classic example is Keat's 'La Belle Dame sans Merci'; the poet's agonized mind has palpably fused Fanny Brawne and Consumption in a single image, yet his own comments at the time (and his revisions are even more symptomatic) seem to show him quite unaware of this at a conscious level.

Usually these same critics (again with Robert Graves among the most emphatic) downright deny the same to be true of prose, that the roots of a prose piece ever run right down "under the threshold" as poetry does. But why? If an imaginative prose work has also insisted on being written – in its humbler way yet still just as irresistibly as a hen's egg insists on being laid – why must the novelist's compulsion be assumed to differ in kind from the poet's? An almost instantaneous flash of lightning and the steady illumination of a lamp are both electric light.

Mostly these multiple generating tensions are private and personal, like Keats's; and in this field, I should probably be the last to know even today what private neuroses of my own saw themselves reflected in these twin symbols of ship and hurricane, or constructed this varied picture of men enduring prolonged inanimate danger to be their escape hatch. But tensions can also derive from the situation of a whole society, and it is here that I think I do begin to see daylight.

For the period when this hurricane story reached and so instantly obsessed me was those early 1930s when the fading smell of remembered death in Britain was just beginning to be replaced by a new stench that was death prefigured. War, we had thought till then, was so safely behind us – the Great War, the "war to end all wars"; for more than 12 years we had been believing that with this final holocaust civilized man had worked war right out of his system. Indeed to many it had seemed an overinsurance that we had even bothered to set up a League of Nations at all, with adequate powers to withstand any risk of war in the impossible event that risk arose! When, step by step, that old postwar world was changed under our eyes into a new prewar one, how *could* we believe it? Reason forbade (for in really important matters Reason always is nine parts wishful thinking).

In 1931, Japan invaded Manchuria and the League failed to stop it. In 1933, Hitler came to power and began to rearm. The next year, his abortive coup in Austria meant that henceforth Mussolini was needed on the Brenner Pass, and Italian designs on Abyssinia had to be winked at. But in Manchuria, we told ourselves, white men weren't involved (and yellow men are a different species from ours – don't quite count). As for Germany rearming, surely she'd a right to resume her place among the Powers, and this would content her? Abyssinia involved only one European nation, so still hardly counted. Spain, then, where white men did fight each other? We were knowing enough Freudians by now to see Spain as a grim football ground where (for the better security of world peace) the Communist and Facist Powers could sublimate in semiprivate.

Right till the end all 10 parts of Reason went on telling us the final cataclysm would be dodged. Even in the summer of 1938, when Chamberlain waved "Peace in Our Time" in our faces, most of us believed him – or thought we did. "Or *thought* we did" – for that is the point I am making, that all this time, the bottoms of our minds knew better; that in our bones we had foreseen from the very beginning this hurricane of preternatural power which no maneuvering could dodge. Under this threshold of consciousness we were well aware that it would prove worse than even imagination could envisage but that we should endure, somehow reviving in ourselves that trust in stubbornness and Providence supposedly long since leached out.

When Reason plays the deaf adder – one ear in the sand and her tail plugging the other – then only symbol can serve; and a true-life story serves best of all as symbol, since even the inward censor has to admit its "truth". Moreover, the text bristles with clues (which is typical of the workings of the subconscious): for example, how could I have written even that first page of the book without recognizing what my "ship" really stood for? Certainly no dream-analyst could.

Of course, had this been allegory and a conscious attempt to foretell the future couched in the terms of allegory, then I could claim to be a prophet of no mean rank: for little ingenuity would be needed to read into the story not only a foretelling of the onset of the war and its violence but even details of its future course – right down to the final *American* salvage ship! But that would be to misread it entirely, since this is not allegory at all but symbol; and symbol (in the dream sense) is never concerned primarily with the future *qua* future but with a much more timeless kind of truth.

All the same, this brings me to my final point: my symbol's eventual impact on my readers.

Till now, we have been concerned only with those motions in the writer's mind which went to make the book. But our initial premise can be applied also to those motions in the reader's mind to which a poem or a book gives rise. For where some tension in the writer's mind has eased itself in symbol, then that symbol may couple itself to a like tension in the reader or even (for that is the ambiguous nature of symbol) to some wholly different one. Indeed, perhaps the real reason we like reading is to have our therapeutic dreaming supplied us, thus, from outside.

It follows that at times of exceptionally deliberate self-deception people tend to shun all poetry and fiction; indeed it is symptomatic of a fear of the naked truth to prefer nonfiction.

From these last two paragraphs, what happened when the book first appeared, and again a little later, can perhaps be imagined. For it was published in 1938. The literary notices it got could hardly have been better, but initially it failed entirely to excite the general reader as, nine years earlier, *A High Wind in Jamaica* had done. For this was Munich-time, and people had something other than mere novels to think about – or supposed they had; and anyway, here was Chamberlain back from Germany with the blessed news that the hurricane *had* been dodged!

Thus initial sales were merely respectable. But when war after all did come and disaster followed disaster, something rather curious happened. Without being any more talked-about than before (for I doubt if readers knew why they were reading it any more than the writer had known why he wrote it), the book became more and more widely read. When at last war was over and the British publisher checked his sales figures, he rubbed his eyes: he could hardly believe that in fact his sales of this book by that time had actually outstripped his total sales of the far more widely talked-of-earlier one – in spite of paper-rationing and all.

So let me sum up, thus: I believe the theme of this book and of the "historical novel of my own times" I am engaged on now to be fundamentally the same. But what *The Fox in the Attic* (and the succeeding volumes still to come) looks at consciously with hindsight, *In Hazard* had already looked at 30 years ago quite unconsciously – with foresight.

1966

On *The Human Predicament*

We all have to live with – and in – our times: we are all atoms of History; but there are two special aspects affecting the writer which do not so much bother his fellows.

The first is "engagement": the problem which so bedevilled the poets of the 'thirties. Ought a writer, lively-minded and prone perhaps to enthusiasms, to espouse political causes and use his gifts in their service? Well . . . *I* have carefully kept out of politics. A writer's gifts are peculiar. He may be the finest – say, lyric poet, in the world; yet his judgement on immediate political issues may be worth no more than his neighbour's. He is fit for a voter but not for a leader – and he will be some sort of leader willy-nilly once he starts to propagandize: his technique and his reputation will give his opinions more weight than they are worth. That is why I have kept out of politics – not for lack of opinions.

In any case, a writer's proper power and influence differ in kind from the politician's. Pure literary power has no constraint in it, no dissenting minority which is forced to toe the line: every reader who accepts it does so of his own free will. It is, in kind, a copy of the power God uses over us.

The second problem is subtler. Should the writer write *overtly* about his own historical times? Should he, like the bard of the *Gododdin,* a non-combatant, record the battle for future generations, and make its issues clearer, perhaps, to his own? It depends upon the writer. Jane Austen wrote about the period of Waterloo but never mentioned the battle – and Jane Austen was right. On the other hand, Homer wrote about Troy – and Homer was right! It depends too on the "times": whether they demand putting on record, as the barbarous Saxon destruction of Britain seemed to demand in the days of Aneurin and Llywarch Hen, and the fall of Troy demanded of Homer. There is no one answer for every writer: it depends on his "call".

It was somewhere in the middle of the Second World War that it suddenly struck me with force: here was I, a lifelong writer – indeed from earliest childhood I never dreamt of anything else – here was I, witnessing one of the most important, dramatic and critical periods in human history! I should be false to my "call" unless I took this theme for my work. For even had I had the pen of a Homer, what more could I ask as theme for a new *Iliad* than this long seige of Hitler's "Citadel-Europe"? And later, was any incursion from Olympus into human affairs ever more dramatic than that *diabolus ex machina,* that devil-out-of-a-machine at Hiroshima and Nagasaki – that devil which one well knew having once made his incursion must hold the stage for ever?

The decision had come like a thunderclap: pondering how to carry it out took me ten years. First, I had to let the thing recede a bit to get it in focus. Then, what kind of book should I write – prose or poetry? History or fiction – or both? I rejected many solutions before accepting this "historical novel of my own times" as the answer. Next, what period had to be covered? I had first intended to write of the war only: it was not until the war receded in time that I realised I had to get back to the beginnings of Nazism. Again, how wide must my canvas be? Should I picture the scene from a single viewpoint or wander all over the world; was my job to picture the changing face – and soul – of the whole of mankind, or my countrymen only?

Ten years . . . Meanwhile, I had to make a living out of film-scripts and so on; but the major affair was never right out of my mind. And in 1955 I began writing.

After all this talk of "ten years", it may surprise you to hear that the work is not even now consciously planned. I prepared no synopsis: I just cannot write that way. If you ask what will happen next, I cannot tell you. All the same, nothing I write is haphazard: the planning goes on all right, in minute detail – but out of sight somewhere, under the "threshold": it only surfaces into consciousness with the pen in my hand. The history, of course, is "given" – I cannot help knowing how that will turn out: but on the fictive side I know even less, at any given moment, what is going to happen next than I know in my own daily life. Things take me by surprise just as much as the reader: the future is a real future in the sense that it is *hidden*.

For me writing can never be, like a piece of carpentry, done from a blue-print: it has to grow – like a tree.

You may say that such writing is bound to be formless: but is it? After all, a tree grows from the roots: but would you call a tree "formless"? The form of every leaf and twig is already laid down in the seed . . . the forester plants it in a picked spot, and tends it and prunes it . . .

Six years ago I sat down at last with a blank sheet in front of me. I was sitting in the sunny garden of a village inn in southern Spain. There were foreign voices all round me; and four feet away a party of children hung on the railings and stared straight into my face . . . But what my mind's eye saw suddenly was a West Wales sea-marsh, a windless damp afternoon . . . I saw two figures approaching – I had not the least idea who they were, but as they loomed nearer out of the mist I suddenly saw with a shock what one of them had on his shoulder. And out of that the whole story grew, spreading and ramifying out of those two lonely figures and the burden one of them carried.

1961

II
On Fiction

Under the Nose and Under the Skin

In a certain country in North Africa, where I spend a good deal of my time, I know of two Englishmen. Both have played an important part in the history of that country, and both have somehow survived for twenty years or so a series of adventures which you would have expected to have sent them under the soil before they had been in the country a month.

Now these two men – charming as they both are – are not very good friends, and the reason is perhaps a surprising one. One of them is one of the best story-tellers I have ever met. He has a brilliant, agile and receptive mind. Nothing escapes his notice, whether it be matters of high policy, or somebody about to shoot him in the back, or the joke of some old market woman. I would happily sit up three whole days and nights listening to his stories. The other, no less fine a character, no less brave, and no less successful, has the mental hide of a hippopotamus. Nothing that happens to him seems to penetrate. And he is as incapable of telling a story as if he were dumb. For instance, I happened to know that he had once fled across the desert for three weeks practically without food or water, pursued by a whole regiment of Arabs. I asked him about this; and he seemed pleased to be asked. He racked his brains for something to say; at last he said it.

"I was very hungry," he said. Then he paused for a while and added emphatically, "I was very hungry indeed."

That was all I ever in my life got out of him about his adventures. This was not through any unwillingness to talk. He was bitterly jealous of his rival's reputation as a story-teller, and full of hints as to what tales he could tell if invited. I think, myself, it was because he had had no adventures, whatever the outside world might think to the contrary. Bullets, poison, and hairbreadth escapes were no more to him than typewriters, telephones and adding up accounts to somebody in an office; and he was as little able to describe them as the average clerk would be to give a vivid account of his life to someone who knew nothing about it. It is a truism that none but adventurers have adventures, but because it is a truism it is none the less true. Why, I have known an old prospector, who was in all the early Australian gold rushes, who lived alone among cannibals for years in his pursuit of hidden metals, and yet who looked on this as the most humdrum method of making a living, and thought it would be the wildest adventure to come to London and earn his living writing for the papers! Now this man was, as a matter of fact, a born writer; but the things he liked to write about in his lonely tent in the bush were the cocks and hens in an English farmyard, or old English maiden ladies in English villas – and moreover, he wrote about them very well.

That may perhaps surprise you. People generally suppose that a writer naturally writes best about what is under his nose, and they even suspect him of being a cheat and a charlatan if he insists upon writing about something else. I do not propose to admit that I am a cheat and a charlatan, but I must confess that I always find it next to impossible to write about what is under my nose. When I go to strange places – when I live among Arabs in Morocco, or among politicians in the Balkans, or in a shack in the woods in America, or the foc'sle of a sailing vessel, or wherever else from time to time I happen to find myself – people always seem to imagine that I am doing it in search of something to write about. Actually the opposite seems to be the case. I seem to find it easier to write about places that I haven't been to than places to which I have been. So much so that when I came to write a novel I found myself compelled to set it in the West Indies – where I have never been; to make the chief character a little girl – and I have never in my life been a little girl; to make the other important characters pirates – one of the few professions I have never attempted; and then to make it all happen forty years before I was born.

Now this is not quite as absurd as it sounds, and I hope you will not think I am becoming too technical if I tell you a little how a writer's mind works. In the first place the material of a book consists of two parts. There is the part which the reader knows about, the part, that is to say, which the writer puts into his book. But there is another part equally important which most readers do not realise to exist: the part, I mean, which he leaves out. That part consists of everything else the writer knows or has experienced, and the reason it is important is this:- Suppose, shall we say, you tell somebody that today has been a hot day. That does not mean that you only know about heat. If you only knew about heat and had never experienced a cold day in your life, you would not know whether it was a hot day or not. And just supposing, for the sake of argument, that I was successful in that novel in describing the tropics, I should put it down myself to my intimate acquaintance, not with the tropics but with their opposite; with the cold and drizzle of the English climate! Now paradoxical as all this sounds, I think it is true, and true in far more complicated ways than the example I have given.

Many writers advise young recruits to their profession to write about their own surroundings, to write about what is under their noses. There are, of course, plenty of writers who do write best about what is under their noses, I am not denying that. But if they do, it is most important that they should not only see what is under their noses. Mr. Sinclair Lewis, for instance, the author of *Main Street* and *Babbitt,* writes about what is under *his* nose, namely, life in the Middle West of America; but I doubt very much if he could have done it if he had not experienced the very different life of an American university, if he had not travelled, as he has, in England and France and Italy, and other places as unlike the Middle West as could be found. While you all know, of course, that when Mr. Arnold Bennett wrote that magnificent study of poverty in Central London, *Riceyman Steps,* he was already a rich man living in the West End, a familiar figure at first nights and society dinner tables.

No, what writers really write about is not so much what is under their noses as what is under their skins; and that they can no more help than a hen can help laying an egg. In that sense all books are autobiographical, even ones which appear to be the opposite. And for a novel to be autobiographical in that sense means not, as is generally supposed, that one of the characters is to be identified with the author, and the others are portraits or caricatures of his friends and enemies; it means that *all* the characters are the author − or rather, that each is one part of the author; and that they are working out some problem, often in allegory which, whether he knows it or not, is dividing his mind at the time.

I hope you will forgive me for having talked so long about authors, a tribe of mankind in whom I am sure you take much less interest than in Arabs and Eskimos. After all, there is very little reason why you should be interested in them. It is just as reasonable to enjoy reading books without wanting to know how they are written, as it is to enjoy eating spinach without wanting to know what chemical fertilisers are most valuable in the cultivation of the spinach-plant. But what I have said does not by any means apply only to authors; it applies, if you stop to think about it, to everybody. How much do you know, you yourself, of what goes on under your nose? When you go to the station in the morning I wonder if you really know much more about the thrilling journey than my friend in North Africa knew about his escapes across the desert! So, if you are sometimes tired of the life you live and wish you were a South Sea pearl fisher, or a millionaire, or a film star, it may perhaps be comforting to think that quite possibly you yourself know more about the life of a pearl fisher, or millionaire, or a film star, than they know themselves.

In fact, you may even be thankful that you are saved from that ignorance of these exciting ways of living which springs from the hopeless handicap of living them.

The Listener
10th June, 1931

The Writer's Duty

Some English writers recently sent to Moscow a budget of questions about the profession of letters in Russia. The leading Soviet writers discussed the questions very carefully in committee; and then sent separate, detailed answers. Questions and answers together have been published as a pamphlet. The replies are unquestionably authentic, and they seem to me to be transparently honest. Certainly no one could take them for mere Ministry hand-outs. But this only shows the more clearly what a chasm today divides the writers of Soviet Russia from those of the West. The pamphlet provides each side with a telescope, if you like; through it the other side can be seen, across that chasm, more distinctly: but it provides no bridge on which they can meet.

For the big question, of course, the question never quite formulated in this questionnaire but yet underlying most of it, is this: How can you Russian writers bear the constriction of writing only upon those subjects which the Soviet State wishes you to write upon, and of expressing only those opinions which the State wishes you to express? And the burden of the Russian reply is this: How could any writer prefer to waste his time on trivialities when he is offered subjects of such importance, and how could he want to express opinions other than those he knows to be true?

I can see no other analogy than that of religion. After all, wouldn't you have got much the same answer if you put similar questions to writers (and painters) in the devout days of Christendom? Suppose you had suggested to Giotto, for instance, that it must gravely handicap his art to have to paint nothing but sacred subjects? Or suppose you had asked Bunyan how he reconciled his conscience with strict adherence to Christian doctrine in everything he wrote?

Thus we arrive at a paradox. The Soviet writer, it would appear, feels every bit as free as we do – free, that is to say, to write what he wants to write. He does not want to utter a literature outside the prescribed range of Marxist-Leninist-Stalinism any more than the devout Catholic wishes to be free to utter heresy, the rationalist to talk gibberish, or the normal writer of any country to publish obscenities. He cannot understand such a wish; nor can he regard it as innocent. For he does not draw the distinction we draw between pure literature and propaganda. For him, all literature is propaganda: if not open, then secret: and if secret, then hostile. Marjorie Bowen asked a question bearing upon this. "Pure literature?" said her respondent: "The mistake lies in supposing that any such thing as pure literature exists." Miss Bowen had instanced Walter de la Mare. The implication of the Russian reply is, of course, that Mr. de la Mare's poetry is a deliberate attempt to distract our minds away from the perpetual contemplation of the necessity of social revolution, and that is just Mr. de la Mare's subtle way of trying to prevent the revolution taking place. Whether conscious of his motive or not, he can have none other!

Thus the Russian writer, it seems, can devote himself to propaganda with his whole heart, with no sense of conflicting loyalties. Lucky fellow! He has gotten himself back to the condition of Adam before the Fall. But for us, who make our constant diet of the Forbidden Fruit, things are not so easy. Incertitude is the price that must be paid for the open mind. Where then lies *our* duty towards a world in conflict? The pen, they tell us, is mightier than the sword: but does that mean it should be used merely for the same purpose – to do battle with?

It is a useful precept, when searching for the truth in rather difficult ground, that time spent in clearing away possible sources of mis-conception is time well spent. That distinction between pure literature and propaganda – for whatever the Russian may think about it, to our minds the distinction is a real one: but are we not perhaps inclined to fall into the opposite error – to assume that the propagandist is merely an artist who has taken the wrong turning? No: they are, I believe, two separate beings, the pure artist and the pure propagandist: both legitimate. It is a question of intention.

Let me take the case of that gifted novelist, Arthur Koestler – I choose him because we have discussed the question exhaustively together over the supper-table into the small hours, he and I, so I feel pretty confident that I am not misrepresenting him. Koestler is primarily a politician. Politics are his principal study, the very fabric of his life, the object of his being. He wants to move people in a particular political direction. For that purpose he finds the novel a very useful tool: so he uses it. He uses it with great skill: but his intention places him poles apart from the pure novelist. For my part (as I told Koestler), if I were to introduce political ideas into a novel, my intention would be the opposite of his: the politics would be the means, the novel the end. I would introduce them merely because they were material necessary to the story I had to tell. That is a totally different kettle of fish.

In considering the writer's duty, therefore, let us be clear about this: we rule out the author who is not primarily a writer, but primarily an advocate using the form of literature as his medium of persuasion. It is the more difficult problem of that curious but not wholly fabulous creature, the pure writer, with which we are concerned. Where does his duty lie, in this world of upheaval? He does not suffer from any lack of people ready to tell him, the Lord knows! Politicians and activists generally are well aware how useful his technical skill could be to them, if only he would put himself at their command. He has no right, they say, to stand aside. Democracy means government by the people – by *all* the people: no single citizen, they argue, has the right to stand out, to refuse to shoulder with all his might a share of the political burden. Surely the inter-war years, when the ordinary man neglected politics till politics took their tremendous revenge on him, should be a lesson to you – yes, even to *you* in your "Ivory Tower"!

I think the answer to that argument is clear. You should say to the politician, Who are you talking to, please? Are you addressing me as John Citizen, or as John Novelist? As John Citizen I admit all you say: it is my duty to enter into politics, at least as far as the polling booth. Or even more perhaps; if I have leisure it may even be my duty to address envelopes at your election headquarters. But it is only my leisure you have any call on, not my professional skill. You don't expect the doctor to exercise his professional skill on your behalf, to cure your friends and poison your enemies: why do you expect me to use mine? John Citizen says, Yes. But John Novelist says, No.

"But my dear chap", says the politician, "I don't understand you. If you are in sympathy with my aims, why aren't you prepared to use your particular gifts in support of them? Why do you refuse to do more than any Tom, Dick or Harry can do?" That plea is rather harder to answer, because to answer it properly requires modesty, and we writers I am afraid are not always as modest as we should be. But I think the answer ought to be this: One reason I refuse, my good Sir, is because so far as politics are concerned a "Tom-Dick-or-Harry" is all I am! I think you are right, and will vote for you: but my friend next door, a soldier on leave, thinks you are wrong and will vote against you. Neither he nor I is an expert politician. Why should my opinion be worth so much more than his, that I should presume to bag you a thousand votes against his one? Is that democratic? You don't encourage him, the soldier, to bring his machine-gun into politics: why should I be allowed to bring that deadly weapon, my pen?

The navigator in the North Atlantic, if he sees a pretty little crest of ice glittering in the sunlight, will give it a wide berth. For he knows that a little ice showing above the surface betokens a big berg below, and he is in danger of shipwreck. Likewise if you see a small piece of genuine modesty showing above the surface of a man's character you should beware: for it surely betokens a solid mass of genuine pride beneath. At this stage, then, the politician will be well advised to sheer off. For he runs the risk of driving head-on into something very hard indeed – the writer's pride in his calling.

Up to now the writer has only pleaded the advantage to politics if he keeps his hands off: that by interfering he is likely to do more harm than good. He has not said what is at the bottom of his mind: that the creation of a work of literature is of greater importance in the long run than any political victory. "Ivory Tower" indeed! That was a witless sneer. It implies that the writer writes only for himself. But if he were creating something for his own sole delight, why should he bother to put it into words; why not be content with easy reverie? Why use words, the very stuff of communication (and awkward stuff to handle, at that)? Man – to supplement Aristotle – may be defined as a communicative animal: and the writer is not inhuman, he is very man of very man. Again, if utmost communication were not the very essence of his calling, why should he use the written word? Writing is a device to bottle knowledge and feeling, so that they can be transmitted across distances of space and down the ages.

The influence of the politician, of every activist, is limited by the period, the place, and the political system into which he is born. His actions are little more than reflexes aroused by the circumstances in which he finds himself. No such limits are imposed on the influence of the writer. Neither space nor time confines him. Is he then to abandon the unlimited for the limited, the substance of his power for the shadow? Again, compare the very nature of these two kinds of power. It is the nature of a politicians's power that it is imposed on some people at least who are unwilling: that is its imperfection. Not so the writer: every person who accepts his power does so of his own free will. Every single one! None is compelled. In that he is copying God rather than the princes of this world.

Wherein then lies the core of the writer's duty – what is it that he has to communicate? Is it new answers to old riddles? No, that is the politician's business, the propagandist's. Rather it lies in the framing of new riddles, posing new questions. In that too he works in imitation of his Maker, Whose every word to man is – not an answer, but a question.

* * *

Now let me tell you a story. Two men were walking by the side of a lake, disputing which of them could do the more to change the landscape around them. The first – a big, muscular fellow – tore up the biggest boulders he could lift, and heaved them into the water. The splashes were loud, indeed terrific; and waves fanned out rapidly from them: but as rapidly died away, the further they fanned from the centre of the commotion. All the other man did was to take out of his pocket a handful of acorns, and scatter them on the turf as he walked.

The Listener
22nd July, 1948

The Novel Behind Your Eyes

I. Literature and the plastic arts

No student of literature can avoid facing the undoubted analogy between literature and the plastic arts. So strong is this analogy, that the very language of conventional literary criticism is constantly emphasising it. We talk of the "form" of a work of literature, its "light and shade", its "colour", its "texture", its "atmospheric effects", its "solidity": as if it was a work of art presented to the physical eye. But there is one fundamental difference between literature and plastic art which cannot be too strongly stressed. *A work of literature has an added dimension, the dimension of time.* The impact of plastic art is virtually simultaneous; the impact of language has duration, a progression from past to future. The reader is as it were a "present moment", a moving point passing from the beginning of a work to the end, not a fixed point to which the whole work is present together in apprehension.

True, we may look at a picture for more than an instant – we may look at it for several minutes, during which its effect upon us may grow: we may go back and look at it again and again and find something fresh in it every time: but that is not the same thing, because this duration is not inherent in the *nature* of its impact. Moreover, it is completely out of the artist's control: he cannot dictate "You will first see this effect, then that". But the impact of even the shortest poem is essentially an ordered sequence of effects, and the order in which he presents his words to us. You can see this even in a single line of poetry; take Keats's lines, for instance:

> Magic casements opening on the foam
> Of perilous seas in fairy lands forlorn.

The opening shock of so strange a juncture – romantic epithet and everyday noun – as "Magic casements": the relaxation of pressure in "opening on the foam" (foam seen from a safe vantage point, as it were): and then the second and final over-throwing thrust – I am using metaphors from wrestling – of "perilous seas in fairy lands" . . . *perilous* seas that carry the reader drowning in their surges to "fairy lands forlorn": *forlorn* . . . "the very word is like a bell"; and so on. It is the order in which these effects are presented to the reader, even more than the power of the effects themselves, which prostrates resistance. It is as a linked succession of experiences that they have meaning. One might indeed say that the poet is a true native of four-dimensional space, the space-time continuum! His control of the three dimensions of Euclidean space is vague, perhaps, where the painter's or sculptor's is precise: but his control of the temporal dimension is precise where theirs is virtually non-existent.

Now poetry is literature *par excellence:* the finest flower of the composite meanings of language. There the problem of how words mean may be studied in the purest and intensest form. Nevertheless, it is particularly germane to study the "meaning" – that is to say, the effect on the reader – of the long novel.

Indeed there are two reasons.

First: if duration is the distinguishing characteristic of literature – distinguishing it from the plastic arts, that is – then the long novel enables us to study this characteristic in its most marked form.

Second: we recognise that there are two meanings of "meaning" – "meaning" in the sense of what passes from the poet's mind into the poem, which I term "Poetic", and "meaning" in the sense of what passes from the poem into the reader, which I term "Rhetoric". Now, because of its *extended* duration we find in the long novel these two kinds of meaning far more widely contrasted than elsewhere.

In the case of a short poem, particularly if we learn it by heart, we can perhaps say that the whole effect of the poem is present in the mind at one time. But in the case of a novel no one that I have ever met has learnt a novel by heart, or indeed has any but the haziest recollection of it when he has finished reading.

The page you are actually reading – that is vivid enough to you perhaps; partly it derives its effect from what you have read already (and similarly it will contribute its effect to what you are going to read): but what you *have* read – apart, that is to say, from this latent effect on what you are reading – has already gone from you. Has gone all vague and indistinct and misty; and misremembered too, as well as forgotten. Things in it loom all out of proportion, like figures in a mist when only the path under your feet is clear and the path behind you is as much hidden as the path in front. And when you come to the end, when you actually close the book, what really remains in your mind? What ''organic unity'' whose value is greater than the value of the sum of its parts?

What then becomes of that analogy with the plastic arts, that ''form'' of the well-composed novel which literary critics like to talk about? Surely when they analyse the ''form'' of a novel for us, and set it down perhaps in a half-page synopsis for us to read and master, they are using the wrong approach altogether! For they are leaving out the most important characteristic of all – the novel's *length,* and the relativity of the human memory. They are presenting for apprehension together effects which were never intended to be apprehended together but in sequence – and perhaps so much separated in time, that one would have been almost entirely forgotten before the other is presented. Thus is comes about that usually the last person to recognise such a synopsis is somebody who has read the book! For it is not *the novel behind his eyes*.

It is very necessary to make this point, because even so perspicacious a critic as Percy Lubbock, recognising this difficulty (or rather, impossibility) of holding a whole novel in the mind at one time, deplores it as being an unfortunate weakness in the critic instead of being the very *essence* of the experience we call reading: whereas in actuality it is characteristic of that experience that the reader moves through his experience of the novel behind his eyes as he moves through life – a present moment, moving always from a partially-remembered past towards a partially-foreseeable future.

II. Why do we read novels?

In the proper days of the last century, novel-reading was looked on for the most part as an idle occupation and it was considered the height of depravity to indulge in it before lunch-time. It was almost as bad as drinking whisky at breakfast. Nowadays we rate novel-reading a little higher than that. The purely anodyne novel is, of course, still with us – the novel we read for no other purpose than ''to take us out of ourselves'', to forget our troubles (and, even more, to forget our duties). That is not the kind of novel I am concerned with here, however. Let us ask ourselves what we get out of novel-reading, what *good* does it do?

There are two kinds of this "good": or, perhaps I should rather say, two levels.

First: throughout our lives we learn by direct experience, by our success and failure in meeting the situations which arise between our environment and the "opposing self" (as Lionel Trilling calls it) which faces it. But in any given lifetime this direct kind of experience is inevitably limited: and our failures moreover are damaging to us personally. But the novel enormously widens our experience, enables us vicariously to live an hundred lives as well as our own and moreover to "experience" failures without any risk of damage to ourselves. In this way the novel provides an important part of that pool of human knowledge on which we can all with advantage draw. Indeed I have heard it suggested that the best possible armoury for a Marriage Guidance Clinic would be a selected shelf of novels!

But the novel can do a great deal more for us than that.

Let me remind you of certain concepts of Dr. I.A. Richards. He speaks of "that growth which is the mind's endless endeavour to order itself", and again of the mind as "a connecting organ which works only by connecting". Novels not only offer us vicarious experience, similar to the direct experience of our daily lives but wider – which is "knowledge": they offer us *new connections* which transcend experience; and that is "wisdom". For they open to us a whole realm of "connecting" which it is impossible, by reason of the laws of the physical universe, for direct experience ever to give us.

This is perhaps a hard saying, so let me try to explain something of what I mean by an example. The story of a novel, of course, has an *internal* duration quite distinct from its *external* duration – the duration of the action it portrays (whether like *War and Peace,* it covers fifteen years of history or, like one of Virginia Woolf's books, a single day). In a chronicle – in a diary, for example, where every day is given equal space, or such a publication as the Annual Register, where each year is given a volume of equal length – the two time-scales, internal and external, are so calibrated that roughly speaking they march together. But between the two time-scales – the internal and external – of a novel, there is no such congruence. You can't say "This page I am reading details the events of exactly a week; if I turn on 52 pages, therefore, I shall find the hero a year older". 52 pages ahead we may even find, on the *internal* scale, that he is a year younger, or even that he has not yet been born! We may find ourselves at his parents' wedding! In short, the "duration" of a novel is utterly divorced from the "duration" of the physical living it recounts. It can go slow or fast in relation to physical events, it can even go backwards as well as forwards. In short, the novel can so *reshuffle* physical space and time as to offer the mind "connections" of a kind absolutely impossible to physical experience.

Let me remind you what Dr. Richards says about language: words are not "a thin, but better-than-nothing, substitute for real experience, – language, well-used, is a *completion* and does what the intuitions of sensation by themselves cannot do. Words are the meeting points at which regions of experience which can never combine in sensation or intuition, come together. They are the occasion and the means of that growth which is the mind's endless endeavour to order itself."

> Come, thou mortal wretch,
> With thy sharp teeth this knot intrinsicate
> Of life at once untie. Poor venomous fool,
> Be angry, and dispatch.

This is an example in the smallest possible compass of meeting-points "at which regions of experience which can never combine in sensation or intuition, come together". In this little passage the meaning is compound of as many and as multiple a complex of connectings as in a Bach fugue. But in this respect the novel is only the poem writ large, because its duration as something read is in no way calibrated to the duration of the physical events it invites us to experience. Because it can linger for pages in a single room, or leap the Atlantic between sentences: crawl through time or rush, at will: leap backwards at will as well as forwards, it too can provide those meeting-points of which Dr. Richards speaks.

In pursuing the idea of "connecting" I have distinguished two aspects of it with regard to the novel. There is what – purely metaphorically – we might call the spatial aspect: the connectings embodied in the polyphonic meaning of a single phrase short enough to impinge on the reader instantaneously, the "meaning" in his mind at any given moment. But because we insist (as we are bound to do) on the time-dimension, that literature unlike art is not a fact but a process, not a being but a becoming, there is a temporal aspect as well. As Murasaki wrote of the novelist's art, nearly a thousand years ago, there is a "so fitting each part of the narrative into the next", a connecting between one meaning and the next meaning – and the next meaning after that. But what are we to call the value we ascribe to it? We are precluded, I feel, from borrowing a term from the static arts and calling it "form", because form suggests permanence and this is in its very essence *change*.

There is one kind of connecting between succeeding events whose validity is generally recognised: a cause-effect chain. If A causes B, we say that B "follows" A. Now the succession of meanings in literature is by no means necessarily a connecting of that kind . . . and yet we feel it to be just as valid as if it was. How are we to explain this? I think we are up against it here. I think we have got to the bottom. I think we have arrived at a primary term.

Let me remind you that many modern students of Ethics, headed by G.E. Moore, believe "Good" to be a primary term, that is a term which can be used to describe other things but cannot itself be explained or defined or described. Like "yellow": you can use "yellow" to describe butter, and flowering gorse, and those yellow sands: but you cannot describe yellowness itself. "By their fruits ye shall know them" – Christ himself came no nearer to describing Goodness than that. We call things yellow because of a certain similarity in the retina's response which they induce. We call things good because of a certain similarity which we recognise in the states of mind which they induce. Similarly I think we call the connectings of the successive meanings of literature "valid" because of what they leave behind when the book is closed and its procession of meanings is passing through the region behind the eyes no longer.

A little while ago I distinguished between "knowledge" and "wisdom". I would say that "wisdom", as an activity of the mind, lies in the polyphonic faculty of connecting of which I have spoken. The novel, then, does not only provide an additional storehouse of knowledge, it enables the mind itself to grow.

1955

Fiction as Truth

"Fiction" derives from a Latin word used of the potter shaping a bowl; yet whilst there is surely nothing deceptive about changing a lump of wet mud into a thing of beauty – and Horace uses this same word of "shaping" a poem – to the public mind today Fiction carries overtones of deception and pretence.

The general reader would probably describe Fiction as "a story we *pretend* is true". What then is he to make of the publishers' negative category, *Non*-fiction? Stuff even its publishers don't pretend is true? Shapeless and meaningless all those biographies and histories, scientific works and schoolbooks which make up four-fifths of modern publishing?

Instinctively, the jargon has chosen correctly which kind of book should wear the positive, which the negative boot. For there is a positive truth peculiar to Fiction, negatived or ignored in all other kinds of writings; and like the moulded clay, a usefulness derived less from substance than from shape. Indeed, the present general retreat of readers from Fiction into a cloud-cuckoo-land of actualities and abstract studies looks like a flight from reality, the flight of an escapist, frivolous generation – and perhaps a doomed one.

Forty years ago a critic could call novelists the spoilt children of the twentieth century: "sanctified personages," he wrote, "as though touched by a divine radiance!" That twentieth century is still with us, but how are those mighty fallen in even their own esteem! One hears uneasy voices saying: "I'm a social reformer really, a Crusader: I wouldn't stoop to Fiction if I hadn't this ideological axe to grind." (Or even, "Me novelist? But I'm pure pornographer!") And as in their own eyes, so in the eyes of others. Today an apparently intelligent man can tell you: "No, I never read *novels*" and plume himself on such proof of his serious-mindedness. Is he totally unaware that he is thereby confessing an unwillingness to face the essential nature of his fellow-men and himself?

For this is no ordinary cloud-cuckoo-land escapism: it masks something much more dire, a solipsist retreat into the fortress of his own 'I am', like that of an autistic child. It is a refusal to face the unpalatable fact about his fellow-men which Fiction might compel him to apprehend, the fact that other people are not "things" but "persons". Not mere machines mass-produced on the genetic assembly line complete with built-in obsolescence, but persons; not things to be studied only from outside and even then in numbers large enough to form categories and classes, not things to be regarded in relation to his own Ego as mere obstacles or raw material or tools – but what Sartre calls the "Other", just as much persons as he is a person himself.

It was the vast failure to learn that lesson which built the gas-ovens. The archetypal non-reader of Fiction was Hitler.

Of course the ability to see deeply into men and women from outside is not peculiar to the novelist. Hitler had that; so had Machiavelli; likewise Freud. What is unique in the novelist's vision differs from this perceptiveness in kind, differs from even the acutest penetration into man as an "object": it is the novelist's ability to station himself inside someone else's innermost "I am" and to look out on the world through other eyes than his own. Not to peer in but to see out, with a rapid series of changes of identity to *be* someone else.

Where the novelist is of supreme importance to mankind is that he can induce this same ability in his reader.

For this is something quite without counterpart in "actual" life. Socially we live more and more like cells in one big organism, semantically and cybernetically we invent more and more means of intellectual conference: yet in our consciousness we remain incommunicable islands. The more we live like sardines in a tin the less can any one sardine inhabit any other sardine. Even in married love we can't become *self*-conscious with the other partner's own "I-ness": we are still each in solitary confinement, only tapping out loving messages on the dividing wall. Only when reading novels (or watching plays and films, to the extent that these too are forms of fiction) do we repeatedly adopt someone else's "I am" for our own, are let out of our solitary cells, think what the other man thinks even while he is thinking it, "identify" with him and feel what he feels.

Churchmen and Humanists can assert that all men are "persons" but cannot bring us to *experience* it like this. Seed with the shallowest of roots, our acceptance of their assertion wilts in the first hot sun of self-interest, whilst the mature fruits of the experience which the novelist communicates to his readers are manifest in history. Penal Reform, for example: and the abolition of Slavery – indubitable fruits of a new nineteenth-century recognition that criminals and even Negroes are not Things but Persons.

Is it irrelevant that our immediate forebears – unlike their own fore-bears, and unlike the present generation – in sheer bulk of reading read more novels than any other kind of book? That apart from the few great poets, the greatest writers of that age gravitated more naturally into novel-writing than into any other kind? For this recognition was not brought about by formal philosophers nor even by the Bible: it came quite simply, to simple people, from reading Fielding and Jane Austen and Dickens – Balzac, Flaubert and Stendhal – Mark Twain – Tolstoy and Dostoevsky.

Today the proportion of Fiction-reading to Non-fiction-reading has dwindled from a preponderance to barely one-fifth: so that even such novelists of the present century as Proust, Henry James and Conrad, James Joyce and Virginia Woolf have been allowed less impact on our own generation. Yet we still rub our eyes at those enormous events of our own lifetime which show so much less that recognition of man's personality than was apparent a century ago! We regard it as of small importance when political tyranny puts the novel in a strait-jacket: but Tyranny knows its importance better than we do. Because tyranny *presupposes* that men are "things' it dare not tolerate Fiction, only lies.

Suppose that Identity itself is questioned in a novel – Genet's *Balcony* hypothesis that the Person may not exist, Beckett's characters stripped down to voices: how can such novelists serve the same benign purpose even if millions did read them? To doubt that is to forget that the business of all Art is to frame questions, not answers: answers are short-lived, forgotten once they've served to point to the new questions which lie beyond them. Even to the scientist the Universe presents itself not as an assertion but a huge question-mark. Earlier novelists framed their questions from the manifestations of identity; Genet, Beckett and others like them from identity's very nature. That is all the difference.

Were you reading, instead of this article, some passage from a novel, you would experience my meaning almost without knowing it. But no form of Non-fiction can do for us what Fiction does. Not even Biography, Fiction's nearest cousin. One speaks of a biography's "subject" though it is rather as an object that he is shown; constructed from external evidence much as the detective constructs his criminal (or your analyst you). The biographer cannot *become* him without breaking out openly into Fiction – as some of them do. . . History is an even remoter abstraction: Biography the perspective drawing of an object, History a diagram of the interaction of such objects.

Science, then? Science, today the prime emanation of the world's thinking skin – of de Chardin's Noösphere, the thin film of conscious intelligent matter stretched over this dead mineral globe – yet in relation to the human condition a further abstraction still, and dangerous because of its impotence in this single field! For Science is compelled to ignore identity completely as something apprehensible only in terms of uniqueness, whereas Science apprehends only classes. Physics in particular looks at the continuum only through the grid of Number. Just as Primitive Man shouted out loud in the face of the Unknown, echo returned his voice and he believed in disembodied spirits, so too the Physicist counts out loud in the face of the Unknown and when it echoes back numbers he believes in certain ultimate numerical constants (that is, if he believes in anything beyond his own *Cogito*).

Indeed I know of only one place to look for anything comparable with Fiction, and that is in the field of religious experience. But here the roles are reversed, for this is the man-in-the-novel become aware of the Novelist! When the mystic looks in on his own very innermost pinpoint "I am", for him that is like looking in through a window and finding himself instead looking out upon landscapes of infinite width: no longer his little "I am" there at all but only the Great "I AM".

Naked to God no apron can hide him: each word of his mouth, each thought of his mind, each lifting of a finger – God knows its meaning even if he doesn't. God is an Eye and the Eye is inside him, God is an Ear and the Ear is inside and the Eye never blinks nor the Ear mishears. No man can look wide-eyed at the depths of his own soul; needing to hood the eyes he turns inwards as from a dazzling by light though this is in fact a dazzling by darkness, by something too dark to bear looking at: yet as an eagle can stare at the brightness of the sun so God stares at even that blackness unblinking.

Still, mystics are few, and for most of us Fiction in one form or another offers our only way of experiencing the identity of others. That identity is the necessary ground of Ethics, and Science is incompetent in the field of Ethics for this very reason, since identity is a concept outside the domain of Number and indivisible into classes. Preaching and proof alike are incapable of inculcating belief in the "Other": that belief can only be born of direct experience – which means, through Fiction.

Suppose we continue, progressively, to turn our backs upon Fiction, letting ourselves lapse into solipsism? We know that for the absolute solipsist the asylum doors gape, perhaps the doors of hell. It is also certain that a mankind in which such solipsists gained the upper hand would be a mankind headed for destruction. We neglect the Novel at our peril.

After all, two rattlesnakes fighting each other wrestle, never use their poison-fangs even as weapons of last resort. If man is even to survive his bomb, he must raise himself at least to the ethical level of rattlesnakes.

Times Saturday Review,
21st March, 1970

III
Four Talks

The Relation of Nationalism to Literature

The title which I have chosen for what I have to say this morning, the Relation of Nationalism to Literature, is a vague one. You will have rightly taken for granted that I meant to discuss a particular case of it. What particularly concerns me under these general terms is the relation which exists, or should exist, between the Welsh writer of to-day and his sense of nationality: between the Welsh writer and his public: and between the Welsh writer and the Welsh Scene around him.

These are intricate questions, and ones which are made no easier by the necessity of examining (even if one cannot answer them) two other questions first. What, in the first place, is a Welsh writer? (Am I, for humble instance, a Welsh writer myself?) And the second question is equally difficult. What is a Welsh author's public? Is he writing solely for his own people, or is he writing with an English public in at least half his eye, if not the whole? Or is he writing not particularly for either, but for that coming African civilisation, perhaps, whose children may one day in their school-rooms puzzle over the literature of both these dead nations?

There is another question which is bound up in this matter of the relation to Nationalism, or rather of Nationality, to Literature; a question so wide and so controversial that we have even less hope of finding an answer to it; the whole question of the relation of a writer and his environment: what it can expect from him, and what he can expect to draw from it.

I have said that we must consider these questions first; but really they are all so interdependent that I am afraid it is going to prove impossible to do as a proper speaker should; to examine one point, draw a definite conclusion from it, dismiss it for good with a kindly pat on the head and turn to the next – ending with a proper peroration and grand summary of conclusions, signed, sealed, and delivered in neatly-labelled packets. At the risk of appearing incoherent and muddled to an audience so critical of style, I am afraid I must proceed on a very different, and inferior, plan; touching on one point, wandering off from it to another, and then to a third, and then wandering back inconsequently to the first. As for the peroration and proper summary of conclusions, I am afraid I cannot promise you any definite conclusions at all; except such as shall appear to you, even if apparently mutually incompatible, implicit in what I shall say.

If we were at an early stage in the world's history, some of these matters would be simple enough. It is true that we Barbarians read the *Iliad* and the *Odyssey* nowadays; but that, when he wrote them, did not concern Homer. He was a Greek, writing for Greeks about Greek affairs. He knew of no other civilisation. There was no literary agent at hand ready to sell for him translation rights into the languages of Chaldea and Crete. The Muse of History was still an infant in the cradle, singing herself to sleep with nursery rhymes; and to Homer, knowing nothing of the civilisations which had gone before him, it probably never occurred that other civilisations and other readers would come after. Thus, though Homer is one of the greatest figures in the literature of the world, he is at the same time a truly national writer.

But in that sense it is impossible for any great writer to be one nowadays. This necessity of literary internationalism is by no means limited to Wales (although it is, of course, emphasised there). No writer nowadays of whatever nation, writes purely and only for his own people, on subjects concerning only them; or is only indebted to the literature of his own people, however wide and rich that may be. Even an English author commonly counts on getting his widest public in America; while a successful book of any nation will probably be translated into fifteen or twenty other languages. Nor does it end with this. There is now a new and indeed universal language into which a book may be translated – the language of the cinema. However imperfect the rendering, this, the writer knows, will carry at least something of his creative thought to millions who will never read the book at all, from China to Peru.

Now, I do not say that in the act of writing he is likely to have this whole vast heterogeneous audience in full view. Almost certainly his main objective will be the readers, or a section of the readers, among his own fellow-countrymen; but at the back of his mind, consciously or unconsciously, the hope of a mundane public does exist, and is bound to some extent to influence his work; while not at the back of his mind but right in the forefront will be present, for information and emulation, the great achievements, not only of his own countrymen, but of the literature of the whole world. For to take again the particular case of the English writer; no one but the most bigoted examiner in the Literature School of a University could really suppose that the sources of English literature are to be found within English literature, or would maintain as true the rigmarole that Beowulf begat Chaucer, and Chaucer begat Shakespeare, and Shakespeare begat Congreve, and Congreve begat James Joyce. The true ancestors of English literature, and even of the English language as spoken and written to-day, are not to be found among the Anglo-Saxons, or among those tribal bards who lisped their numbers in Old High Gothic. These ancestors are really the authors of Greece and Rome, of Palestine, of Italy and France, and Germany and Russia.

If even the English author writes in part at least for foreigners, and if his books have all foreign blood in their veins, it is still more likely that this should be the case with a smaller and less isolated nation. It is unavoidable that an ambitious Welsh author of to-day should write not solely for Welshmen; and I regard it as equally inevitable that he should be deeply steeped in the literature of England and other countries, not only in the early literature of his own – beautiful though some of that is, if exiguous.

I am afraid that the ardent nationalist, the kind at least who hopes for a great modern Welsh literature written by Welshmen who have never left Wales, nor read anything but other Welsh literature; written by Welshmen who know as little of the English language as the infant first styled Prince of Wales himself, and who have no other audience in view but their fellow-countrymen – that kind of nationalist (if he still exists) has at least one invincible opponent to fight: *the clock!* Enthusiasm can do much, and the ability of men of genius can do much; but neither of them have ever succeeded in putting the clock back.

Moreover, it is inevitable, a fact which must be faced and accepted, that among foreign audiences and literatures, one should occupy for the Welshman a disproportionately prominent place. For the parallel I have drawn between the literature of Wales and the literature of England in this matter is not entirely a fair one. The two cases are not quite on a par. No other country, not even France, has ever loomed so large in the history of England, as England has in the history of Wales. Lloegr may be to the Welshman a foreign country; but it is in a special position as such, which distinguishes it in a very special way from all other foreign countries. It is inevitable that the English public on the one hand and English literature on the other should loom, even if only by the laws of perspective, larger in Welsh eyes than those of the rest of Europe put together.

Wales, in short, plays towards England the part (if I may wed two hackneyed metaphors) of a Pious Pelican with a cuckoo, a very large cuckoo, in her nest.

But it is not only in the way of literature that she feeds that cuckoo with blood from her breast. For many centuries she has done so in all the arts of civilisation: in medicine, in engineering, in industry, in religion, and perhaps most noticeably of all in politics. The very existence of a society like the Cymmrodorion, an alliance of the sons of Wales which nevertheless has its headquarters in London, is a witness to it.

There is no point in my attempting to enumerate a long list of names better known to you than me; say them over to yourselves, if you like; but Wales, for example, once gave England her greatest dynasty of kings: and even in the present generation we have seen her give the British Empire, apart from Cabinet Ministers, two Prime Ministers at once. Is the contribution of Hughes to Australia and Lloyd George to the Imperial Parliament, apart from the others, a negligible loss of blood, when given by so small a pelican to so large a cuckoo?

Hitherto my method in viewing the problem has been a purely realistic one. I have been entirely concerned with conditions as they are, and have offered no opinion on what they should be or what they might have been; but it may perhaps at this point be entertaining to venture (if one can do so without trespassing too much on ground already hallowed by Sir George Trevelyan) into this limbo of might have been.

Let us suppose that there had been no England to tempt the most eminent sons of Wales away from their homes. Let us imagine that the Welsh polity was as insulated as Greece was – say at the time of Pericles; and let us imagine that instead of Glyndwr it was Elizabeth Tudor who had ruled from Dolgelley. Might she have laid the foundations of a Welsh World-Empire, do you think, instead of an English one? Or let us come to the present day, and imagine that Mr. Lloyd George, having made himself, when little more than a boy, Tyrant of Criccieth, has captured, with the swift triremes of Portmadoc, those other two ambitious heads of little rival Welsh city-states, the Australian Hughes and Mr. J.H Thomas. As punishment for the wickedness of their politics, he has condemned them to work in chains in the quarries of Festiniog. His army, perhaps, is led by a

General of foreign blood; but one who was born, or at least spent his childhood, at Tremadoc – Lawrence of Arabia.

King Dafydd Lloyd is still a young man; but the cup of his political ambition is full. What other outlet now remains for his energies except to rebuild, from the granite of Moel-y-Gest and Pwllheli, to the plans of Clough Williams-Ellis perhaps, a Criccieth designed to become deservedly the cynosure of the twentieth century civilised world; a miracle of statecraft, of intellect, and of beauty?

Would he have succeeded? Would he have created a Criccieth as glorious as Athens once was? For this comparison is not altogether ridiculous. It is a principle of hydraulics that the narrower the outlet the greater the head of power; and anyone would hesitate to deny outright that it may be also a principle of human energy. Imagine what energy would here have been cooped up in a small space! Mr. Lloyd George might indeed have won himself an even brighter fame as Tyrant of little Criccieth, than he has as Prime Minister of the Imperial Parliament. It might indeed in that case have come about that Criccieth occupied in the history books of the future that glorious position which Athens occupies in ours.

If you are still sceptical, let us imagine the converse. Let us suppose that Greece, early in its history, became a province of the Persian Empire, and that Persia occupied towards it something of the position which England occupies to Wales. You might argue that this would only be throwing open a wider field to the genius of her sons than Athens or Sparta could offer them; but I think what would have happened would be very much more like this. Pericles, aspiring beyond the Chairmanship of the Urban Council of Athens, would have ultimately been lost to sight in some dark corner of the political back-stairs of Sardis. Phidias, an emigrant to the distant metropolis, would have broken his heart executing the portraits of rich Satraps to feed the family he had left behind him. Euripides and Sophocles would have dulled their wits reviewing, at a daric a thousand, for the Median Quarterly; or adapting the stage hits of Egypt to tickle a Persian audience. And what of Aeschylus? Of him no one might ever have heard at all. You will remember that he nearly got knocked on the head at Marathon. Is it too fanciful to suppose, do you think, that if history had taken the course I have suggested, he might have succeeded in doing so – not on his own soil at Marathon, but in a distant desert of Central Asia: serving the Persian, when little more than a school-boy, in some great, but now utterly forgotten, War to End War? A war which, in its result, proved instead a War to End the Younger Generation?

But history is what has happened and is happening, not what might have happened; and it is with conditions as they are to-day that I am at present concerned. If Welsh political nationalism even now achieved its object, and at least a measure of political isolation was attained, it is impossible, under modern conditions, that cultural isolation would follow. It is therefore the realms of pure fancy into which I have been venturing: but nevertheless I have done so in order to illustrate and emphasise a fact. For it is a fact, that it is not the fault of Welsh genius if the national fame of Wales does not to-day stand among the very highest in the world, and perhaps never will. It is the fault of that mischievous and interfering female, History; and hers alone.

I prefaced these remarks which I have the temerity to address to you with the warning that they were likely to be vague and incoherent; and I am afraid the warning has proved a necessary one. I said that the task of drawing conclusions from what I put forward was a task I proposed to leave to you, and I am afraid that what conclusions you may up till now have drawn will hardly be valuable ones, or even the ones I intend. All I appear to have done up to now is to argue that there is no place for nationalism in modern literature, just as there is a diminishing place for it in modern state-craft; even to have hinted that the Welshman should not write for his own people at all, but aim rather at capturing an English public if he has the ability to do so. At the same time I may appear to have suggested rather irrelevantly, or even contradictiously, that if Wales enjoyed political nationalism of the fullest kind her literature and art would have benefited immeasurably.

Neither of these conclusions however do I wish to leave unqualified. In the first place I want to reiterate that I am describing what I see, rather than venturing an opinion on what should be; I have simply stated what no one could deny – that the tendency of the majority of Welshmen of outstanding ability is to face towards England. I have neither praised this nor condemned it. But I do not, if you press me, think it really possible to blame them for it. It is an inevitable corollary of the conditions of modern life.

I now propose to look rather more closely into the results of this leakage of national genius: for, I think we shall find that some at least of them are very curious and interesting.

I think we shall find, if we look carefully and without prejudice at the state of Wales to-day, and search, not in probabilities but in fact, for the cultural results of the present situation of this country – I think we shall find ourselves arriving at a rather unexpected conclusion. I believe it will appear that this loss of many of her men of greatest ability has been not wholly a disadvantage, but in some ways an actual advantage to the national culture of Wales.

This may seem rather a surprising statement. Let me try and make a little clearer what I mean.

In the first place, let me ask you to jettison, at least for the moment, our habitual methods of judging a national culture. For it may be that we have clung too long to the habit of judging a civilisation by its giants. Economists have ceased to judge of the condition of a monarchy by the personal ability and wealth of its monarch; but we still incline to judge the state of art and literature in a country by the eminence of a few men of genius who happen to have been born there, without taking into account the cultural significance or insignificance of its average citizen.

Now if in political theory this has long gone out of fashion, and the greatest good of the greatest number has become an axiom, why should we regard that axiom as inoperative in discussing intellectual values? The English in particular, it seems to me, have been far too content to plume themselves on the few men of pre-eminent genius they have produced; and by allowing their eyes to be dazzled by these stars they fail to observe how low is the average cultural intelligence of England. Once upon a time England produced Shakespeare, and may rightly pride herself on it; but in the present generation alone she has produced sixty millions of people who are very far from being Shakespeare – why, having given birth three hundred years ago to this one pre-eminent dramatist, to-day she can hardly even find an audience for his plays! The Englishman prides himself on Milton and Shelley and Keats, but has no inclination, except perhaps in his green-sick school-days, to write a word of verse on his own account.

We do not altogether consider healthy the political condition of that country whose citizens complacently resign the conduct of their affairs into the hands of a benevolent despot, however able. We are far more inclined nowadays to admire the country where they busy themselves, one and all, even inefficiently, with public affairs; and where they are distrustful of the expert dictator who offers to relieve them of this tiresome business. For what reason, therefore, should we admire the culture of a nation which is willing to leave its literature and art in the hands of a few expert poets and painters? Should we not instead reserve at least some of our praise for a nation which looks on literature and art and music as the concern, not of freaks and experts, but of every man-jack in it?

Now, it is in this intimate concern of the whole nation for the Arts that the value of Welsh culture, as it seems to me, lies. Is it possible to find a reason for it? The pollarded tree grows thicker than her sister whose bare bole lifts her feathery head into the clouds; and I think it is partly, as I have suggested, to this perpetual pollarding of Wales by England, this filching away of many of her most eminent sons, that Wales owes some at least of its unusually wide-spread public interest in the Arts. The Welshman is not able to turn to a few eminent experts, and leave in their hands his politics, his literature, and his music, because those experts are liable at the critical moment to take train for London and leave him in the air. He has therefore to attend to these matters himself.

Nine years ago, I remember asking Colonel Lawrence, now known as Aircraftsman Shaw, why it was that, having laid the foundations of a nation in Arabia, he had left the Arabs and retired to England and obscurity. He told me, without any false modesty, that he had done so in part at least for the benefit of the Arab nation. He might perhaps have won himself a throne, as Rajah Brooke did in Malay; and lifted his Arab subjects, by his own abilities, into a position of importance. But this he felt certain would have been a mistake. The only hope for the Arab nation, once given a fair start as he had given it, was to conduct its own affairs and find its own place in the world; and if time has shown that they were incapable of doing so, it does not show that Lawrence's argument was necessarily false. It only proved unsuccessful because the Arabs of the Hedjaz had not the innate ability. In the average Welsh-man on the other hand – to turn from the world of politics to the world of the Muses – this necessary ability is present. It has grown rather than withered under the necessity for self-reliance. And thus it is one is not surprised in Wales to find a bardic chair as the honoured ornament of any little farm-house kitchen, while one would be extremely surprised to find any equivalent in the same sort of place in England.

I was walking with Robert Graves, once, in the hills behind Harlech. Graves had already then made a name in England and America by his War poetry – was already recognised as one of those experts to whom the English so willingly entrust their poetic affairs. Calling at a cottage, we saw just such a bardic chair. "Who is the poet?" said Graves. "I am", said a young man with a hayrake over his shoulder. "So am I", said Graves; and immediately they sat down together to compare the techniques of poetry in the two languages. All this was without surprise and without self-consciousness on either side. If they had wanted to summon a third poet to their conference, they would probably only have had to call in the shepherd. But imagine (if you can) such a thing happening in England! Imagine, even, an Englishman confessing to a stranger that he was a poet, except from behind the safe barrier of print!

The picture, of course, has its reverse side. The young man may have been a very bad poet. It is quite likely. It may have been that he could only be called a poet at all in a country which had no Shakespeare to put him to the lie. Or he may have been a very good one – a Shakespeare in all but the world-wide glory. Please do not think that I wish to belittle the individual achievements of Welsh poets, or to suggest that an institution such as the National Eisteddfod is unlikely to bring to light work of the greatest value and beauty. All I wish to point out is that, in my opinion, the essence of the Eisteddfod does not lie in this. Literature of value and beauty can come to light by far less cumbersome and expensive means – such, for instance, as being sent by ordinary parcel post to a publisher. No. The chief value of an Eisteddfod, and the peculiar value, in my eyes, of all Welsh culture, lies in the quite unparalleled public interest in literature and art and music which it exemplifies. Is there any other nation in the world whose greatest national gathering is convened for such a purpose? Is there, or has there ever been, or will there ever be another nation whose only titles of honour are conferred for services rendered to the Muses? In short, is there any other nation whose chief national interest, second only to religion, lies in what one may call, in the broad Platonic sense, *"Music"?*

Gentlemen, I may have insisted wearisomely on the fundamental difference between these two kinds of culture – the one, which is to be judged by its single eminences; the other, which is to be judged by its average; and even then not have insisted emphatically enough. For I do believe that they are utterly different in kind; and yet this belief is one to which one comes slowly. I do not think now as I used to (and as anyone naturally would) that the one leads to the other. I have shown how the average may actually be raised by the absence of the best; and in the same way, experience shows that the best does not by any means always flourish most readily where the average is high. If one is to see Welsh culture in its proper light and at its proper worth, I feel that one must accept this radical difference, without implying inferiority or superiority to either kind. They cannot be measured against each other. Each has its own peculiar value.

I have suggested that I did not always hold this opinion. The contrary belief, indeed, once led me to make what experiment showed to be a great mistake. Of that experiment possibly some of you may have heard. I refer to the venture once known as the Portmadoc Players; a venture in the foundation and direction of which I had the honour to be associated with Mr. A.O. Roberts.

After all, when I first came to live in Wales, towards the close of my school-days, living in a little one-roomed cottage at Talsarnau, I came there as a stranger. For though I am Welsh by blood, and Welsh by sympathy, and Welsh now by domicile, I am not Welsh by birth or education: and it is therefore only with the greatest diffidence, as I suggested in my opening words, that I can pretend to being a Welsh author at all. I came to Wales, as I say, a stranger; and one of the first things which struck me was the extraordinary high average of culture in the countryside around me. The tiny hamlet of Llanfrothen (to which I shortly moved) at that time boasted a theatrical company which acted plays in the school-room, written in the Welsh language by the village school-master. Portmadoc, whose population is, I believe, only some-where in the region of three thousand, nevertheless boasted three theatrical companies and an opera company which performed Welsh opera. Even the boat-builder there was a distinguished poet and litterateur: and a railway clerk one of the most famous poets in the country. The very tramps on the roads were prepared to sing for their supper; any school-child could recite with a technique and assurance which are rare indeed among the infant Saxon. It was the custom for the butler of a friend of mine after dinner to play Welsh folk-music on the organ to his master's guests, while the unmusical master served the coffee and liqueurs. At the same tiny hamlet of Llanfrothen a Chairing Eisteddfod was held, amidst the utmost enthusiasm – the sort of enthusiasm that in England would have been reserved for a football match or for a cattle show.

There was no reason to suppose, and it would have been wrong to suppose, that the Glaslyn district was peculiar in all this.

It seemed incredible to me, brought up as I had been in a centripetal culture, that with all this intellectual enthusiasm and all this intellectual ability there should not be, to take the single instance of drama, a National Welsh Theatre which would put the Abbey Theatre at Dublin completely in the shade. If there was not one already, I argued, let one immediately be brought into being. It should be simple enough. A county cricket team is recruited from village cricket, and the team to represent England is chosen from the county teams. The first step, therefore, was to found a district company in some such district as the Glaslyn Valley, recruiting for it the best talent from all the small companies I saw around me. If other districts all over Wales did the same it should only be a matter of time before the second step was taken – the recruiting of a National Company from these companies representing districts.

It was, perhaps, a scheme so charmingly simple that only a very young man could have really believed it would succeed; but I did believe it, and it was in this belief that the Portmadoc Players were founded.

The sequel was not quite what I expected. In the first place, it proved extremely difficult to work in harmony with the existing companies, who insisted on looking upon us as a rival, and were unwilling to believe that our purpose was simply to borrow their actors and give them greater scope, not steal them altogether away. We thus were compelled to pick a temporary cast altogether at random, which we could not pretend really represented the very best talent that the district provided. In the second place, there was no sign of the idea spreading: we saw no other district companies spring into being in other parts with similar objects – and this, of course, was an essential part of the scheme. In the third place, when the whole scheme was still in its cradle, when our cast had only made a single public appearance in one hastily-concocted bill of plays, there came Sir Nigel Playfair's invitation to show ourselves in London.

Looking back, I now think we ought to have refused the invitation. It was altogether outside our original plan of campaign. We made, of course, no pretence to being ourselves a National Company; we were simply a scratch company from the Glaslyn district, and even in our wildest optimism we knew it would be many years before a National Company fit to perform in foreign parts for the honour of Wales could rise from our ashes. On the other hand, there was plainly a lot to be gained by accepting. The cast might learn a lot from their contact with the professional theatrical world. The scheme and its objects would obtain a wide publicity which otherwise we could not hope for – a publicity which might be of the utmost value to the whole campaign. Success, moreover, might encourage the apathetic in our own body. The invitation was premature, plainly; but there was no reason to suppose that, if once refused, it would ever be repeated.

These were some of the considerations which made us decide to accept.

But the result did not turn out as we had hoped. It is true that we received the most cordial and generous support from the London Welsh, for which I can never be grateful enough: it is true that the Portmadoc Players themselves as a dramatic company received most encouraging notices in the press. On the other hand, we were as unable to make the real nature of our scheme clear to the English press as we had been to the local companies. We explained it in interviews, we printed it in our programmes; but with a calm indifference to whatever we might say, the London critics almost without exception insisted on regarding us as a National Welsh Company in being, and compared us (naturally to our disadvantage) with the Irish Players. Perhaps it was a compliment, under the circumstances, that they could possibly have made such a mistake; but it was an exasperating one. It was only natural that Wales should be more resentful of our presumption in apparently pretending to represent her than pleased at what success we obtained. And frankly I think that we obtained more success than we deserved. The performance may have been surprisingly good if all the circumstances are taken into consideration – especially when one realises that our appearance at the Lyric Theatre, Hammersmith, was only our second public appearance on any stage. On the other hand, it was certainly not so good as some of the critics were kind enough to say.

Well, the company returned to Wales with its London laurels; and on its return I resigned, for a variety of reasons, from my share in its management.

In the first place the Portmadoc Players were now, I felt, fully launched; and I did not feel it was fitting, if they were to play their proper part in the history of Welsh drama, that a mongrel such as myself should remain at their head. It was a post which only a pure Welshman ought to fill.

They were, as I thought, now well launched: and the scheme, I thought too optimistically, was well launched with them. One had only, I thought, to sit back and watch the other district companies I hoped for spring up, and the whole movement for a Welsh National Theatre gather momentum.

I had moreover a less altruistic reason for resignation. The organis-ation of the London performance had kept me in London for four or five months and occupied, so unskillful was I at such business, practically my whole time. This prevented me from writing (which is, after all, my main purpose in life): and turned a private purse already empty into a purse heavily in debt. The job of an actor-manager was not one for which nature has fitted me: and once I felt myself no longer necessary, I was not unwilling to quit it and return to writing poetry.

But my whole argument, as I confessed, had been founded from the very beginning on wrong premises. I now believe that the Welsh Theatre is considerable, whether a central National Company ever comes into existence or not. From the point of view of Welsh culture, that is immaterial – or almost so. It is the number and minor excellence of the small companies that are its peculiar characteristic. The dramatic interest and dramatic ability of every Welshman, whether he is acting in a village hall, or conducting a village auction-sale, or simply gesticulating to a friend at a street corner – it is this which is characteristic of the peculiar nature of Welsh culture, rather than any National Company of a few superlatively fine actors that may, or may not, some day carry the fame of Wales into the theatres of Europe and America.

From the point of view of the Welsh dramatist, of course, this absence of a first-class National Company is deplorable. As a dramatist, I should welcome with the utmost enthusiasm any sign of the birth of such a company. No dramatist is ever content with any but the finest possible production, and indeed he is seldom content with that; and it would be little use, as things are at present, for a Welsh Shakespeare to arise and write a Welsh *Hamlet* or a Welsh *Lear*. If he writes anything too ambitious for the village company, he has little hope of adequate production at all. Certainly he cannot expect it in London. It is extra-ordinary how little the Londoner knows about the Welsh. He is familiar on the stage with the Irishman, the Scotsman, the Esquimo and the Negro, but the Welshman might have eyes in the middle of his chest for all the London theatre-goer knows. The Welsh accent has never been employed on the English stage, except rarely and in the most cumberous parody. I found this to my cost, when I wrote a play whose characters were drawn from the countryside around me – the *Comedy of Good and Evil*. It was produced at Oxford and London; there were other productions of it at the Birmingham Repertory Theatre, and at the Abbey Theatre in Dublin. In each case, from every point of view, its Welshness proved a severe handicap to it. Few actors could be found who had any knowledge of the Welsh accent, or any understanding and sympathy for the Welsh character. As a result, a play which I feel sure would have appeared simple enough and clear enough if it had been

performed by Welshmen for Welshmen, seemed wild and incomprehensible when performed by Englishmen for Englishmen; and on this
account came in for exaggerated blame and, paradoxically enough, for
exaggerated praise too.

Perhaps the *Comedy of Good and Evil* is a little difficult for a village
company to undertake. At any rate, I hope that is the reason why,
although what little reputation I have as a Welsh dramatist is almost
entirely founded upon that play, it has never, since I wrote it, received a
single performance within the borders of Wales.

I have argued that these two kinds of culture, the one centripetal and
the other centrifugal, are as incompatible as oil and water: that the
natural corollary of a country without a capital is an art independent of
a few superlatively great artists. What, then, is the Welshman to do,
whose personal ambition overtops the scheme in which he is born? Is he
to be blamed for leaving it, and looking for a place for himself in the
contrary system of England? I think it is only natural for an artist to seek
the widest public that his talents entitle him to. We have seen that he is
doing no harm to Welsh culture by this. Is he therefore to be regarded as
a traitor and outcast, and forfeit the very name of Welshman? This
seems unnecessarily harsh. He may do good service to his country, if his
subject should happen to be the life around him, by making it more
intelligible in the eyes of the outside world. But even if this is not the
case and he chooses some altogether alien subject, he may still remain a
true Welshman if he sees it, as he is bound to see it, through Welsh eyes.
This was the case of many of the Metaphysical Poets of Welsh origin,
for instance, of the seventeenth century.

I have not left myself time, nor is this exactly the occasion on which to
discuss so wide a question as the whole relation of an artist to his
subject. It is one which requires the most careful and exactly detailed
consideration. One cannot summarise it in a few words. I once joined
public issue with Sinclair Lewis on this very point, when he suggested
in an article that the whole duty of an American author was to depict the
American Scene. Do the English upbraid Shakespeare for laying the
scenes of many of his plays in Italy? Do they even upbraid Sir James
Jeans as a bad patriot for taking as his subject the remotest depths of
interstellar space?

Must a writer always write about what is under his nose? Surely it is
more important that what he writes should come from under his skin,
than that what he writes about should come from under his nose? And if
other writers are allowed this freedom without reproach, why should it

be taken for granted that a Welsh writer must write of nothing, and think of nothing, but the obvious superficies of the Welsh Scene around him, whether in praise or satire? If he is a true Welshman, I repeat, and if he writes what comes from under his skin, his writing will be truly Welsh literature – as truly as *Romeo and Juliet* is English literature.

Gentlemen, I am afraid I have treated you rather scurvily this morning. You are accustomed at your meetings to be fed with facts and discoveries, the true bread of scholarship and research. All I have given you has been a rather gaseous hotch-potch of empty ideas and notions, some of them platitudinous, others probably wrong-headed. The art of public-speaking, moreover, is diametrically opposed to the art of writing: I have not, alas! inherited it from my Welsh ancestry: I am unfamiliar with, and inept at it. If it took me three years to write a tolerable novel, it would take me three hundred years to compose a tolerable speech. So I ought, perhaps, to have had the modesty to refuse Sir Vincent Evans' invitation; but the temptation it offered for making your acquaintance was too great. Instead of a peroration, therefore, and grand summary of conclusions, I offer you an apology: that I, who have no claim to call myself a scholar, and so poor a claim even to call myself a Welshman, should have had the temerity to occupy the time of so learned a Welsh Society.

Address delivered at the meeting of the Cymmrodorion Section of the National Eisteddfod (1931) at Powis Hall, U.C. Bangor, on Wednesday 5th August, 1931. Published in the *Transactions* of the Honourable Society of Cymmrodorion – Session 1930-31 (London, 1932).

The Poet and the Scientist

I have a difficult subject to discuss this evening: a subject which so far as I am aware has not before been discussed in modern terms – at least popularly. To deal with it at all adequately would take me at least three hours: and I am going to try and condense it into a quarter of that time. We have a long way to go, so we must travel fast. Instead of proceeding at the proper patient shuffle of a good lecturer, I shall have to take rather long and hurried strides. You must forgive me if I generalise too much and too loosely, and exaggerate: it is impossible not to exaggerate when one has to be brief.

I want to analyse and compare the behaviour of the Physicist and the Poet; for I think the time has come for a new assessment of their relationship.

Between the poet and the scientist themselves there is a good deal of misconception and prejudice: perhaps we had better begin by trying to clear that away. The poet looks on the scientist as at best a logical seeker after the ultimate reality: as at worst a pretentious dry-as-dust fellow, quite tightly confined within the bounds of commonsense. The scientist looks on the poet as a man with a vivid but intrinsically slack mind: at best, a romanticist who can embellish the naked shape of his own discoveries with an irrelevant halo of picturesque language: at worst, a dealer in outworn and hackneyed mist and moonshine.

The poet is unaware that the scientist of today has left the bounds of commonsense far behind: that the kind of mental fusion required in thinking of light (for instance) in terms of both a wave-theory and a quantum-theory at the same time, is a fusion in a close degree similar to those translogical mental fusions which are the common material of his own poetic. The scientist, for his part, sees that the sequences of the poet's thought are little bound by the rigours of pure logic: he does not realise that they are bound by other rigours equally strait, equally cogent, and equally significant.

Neither, if he is quite honest, is prepared to admit the other to be his intellectual equal.

The reason why this mutual misunderstanding is so general is simple. It is very rare that the first-rate in one group comes in contact with, or attempts to understand, the first-rate in the other group. So the scientist judges poets by the second-rate poet: the poet judges scientists by the second-rate scientist. Science has unquestionably its pedants and dry-as-dusts, just as poetry has its poetasters and mongers of stale moonshine. But it is not by these that either should be judged.

Let me take an example of the kind of misunderstanding that arises. Not so very long ago an American scientist of international reputation chose to castigate in print a *soi-disant* poet, who had objected to the "desecration" of the Arizona Desert by electric pylons. So far so good. But then the scientist, in a flood of declamation, told the poet what his poetic attitude ought to be. How his heart should thrill at the romance of modern electrical generation: how he should see, with his mind's eye, the hundred thousand horse-power conveyed by those cables as a hundred thousand prancing steeds, tight-roping on the overhead wire.

The poets amongst you will listen to those instructions with rather a wry smile. For the real pity, of course, is not that poets should fail to visualise a horse-power as a quadrupedal horse, but rather that so many second-rate poets actually *do* think in silly, crude, and hackneyed images of that calibre. Such images indeed have been the stock-in-trade of twopenny poetasters now for many decades: ever since, in fact, some time in the Nineties, Romance (at Kipling's behest) brought up the 9.15.

Can scientists honestly think that the poet is no good except for ornamental puerilities of this sort?

The flood-tide of revolution in physics has slackened somewhat, these last five years: and the time seems ripe to review not only what science in the twentieth century has discovered about the universe, but also what science, in the process, has discovered about itself. For the latter is perhaps the greater revolution of the two.

Science in the nineteenth century was a search for objective truth – a truth that was there to be looked for, like a needle in a bundle of hay, like the murderer in a detective story. The scientist had only to collect the clues: to make those deductions that commonsense approved of: and then, by arguing from them in a matter-of-fact way he was bound to arrive at the solution. Science, to sum up glibly, was "concerned with reality." That position is no longer tenable today. Though few scientists, even, seem to realise it.

But if I am to show that the position is untenable: if I am to argue that the scientist does not discover a truth which is in the Universe, but rather manipulates a truth which he projects upon the Universe, I shall have to do more than merely to review the discoveries of twentieth-century physics. The astronomer, with the micrometer-eyepiece of his telescope, projects a network of fine lines onto the sky, and by that means divides the sky into squares. I shall have to show the nature of the frame, or network, which modern science has projected upon the Universe. To do that we shall have to desert physics, and examine the discrepancies and confusions that exist between applied and abstract mathematics. These two steps are both necessary in turn to the argument.

The world which our ordinary powers of apprehension inhabit, the world of commonsense, is a middle-sized world. Such also was the world of nineteenth-century science. But modern physics has explored, in two directions, greatly beyond that world: it has explored towards the very large, and it has explored towards the very small. It has attempted to study the smallest possible component of matter, the individual electron: and it has also attempted to discover what it can about the largest possible collection of matter, the Universe considered as a whole. On both journeys the search has been guided by a maxim which today is a commonplace of the scientist (though in fact it has been practised by all true poets in all times): the maxim that nothing should be believed which cannot be observed. And the physicist has been led, by that apparently commonplace and unadventurous maxim, to the discovery that in both these directions, both in the very large and the very small, if only the exploration be carried far enough, the rules of commonsense, the laws of the middle-sized world, cease to apply.

We were all taught at school, for instance, that the three angles of a triangle together add up to two right angles: we were taught that this is unescapably true, whatever size the triangle might be. But the physicist says it is not true of triangles enormously large. Again: commonsense would say that it must always be possible to decide whether one event happens before or after another. But the physicist has discovered that if the difference between the velocities of the objects to which these events occur is sufficiently great, one cannot say for certain which happened first. Thirdly: commonsense presumes that any given piece of matter must always either be, or not be, in a given place. Indeed the smaller the piece of matter concerned, commonsense would argue, the more precisely should it be possible to define its position. But the physicist has found that if the piece of matter be small enough: if it be an individual

electron, that is to say: it is not possible to assign it a definite position in space and time at all.

At this stage the modern scientist was faced with a difficulty from which his fathers were comparatively free. The object of science, he believes, is not only the personal discovery of truth: it is also the precise description of truth. But how was he to describe the characteristics of the electron, or of space? His fathers described their discoveries in precise and literal language: but precise and literal language is the language of commonsense: it is a vehicle which cannot be adapted to describing what is beyond commonsense.

Two courses were open to him. If he was to continue to use verbal language at all, it must cease to be precise and literal. If he was to remain precise and literal, he must cease to use verbal language at all.

In actual fact, scientists have adopted both these courses. When they wish to be precise and literal, they describe things not in words but in mathematical symbols. When they wish to use words they are forced – just as Jesus Christ was forced, when he would say the unsayable – into the use of parables.

It is unfortunate however that the scientists themselves (and their hearers even less) did not at once realise what they were doing. Great religious teachers have always realised it, when they spoke in parables, they have done it deliberately. But the scientists did not at first realise it, nor did they do it deliberately. They drifted into it: and only gradually came afterwards to realise what they had done. For instance, the wave-theory of light. This the nineteenth century certainly took to be a literal truth. In everyday life, we were familiar with several different varieties of waves. There are the waves of the sea, for instance. There are the concentric waves which spread out when a pebble is dropped in a pond. There are the waves of sound which spread out when a hammer strikes a gong. The nineteenth-century scientist observed that light too seemed to appear to move in a wave-like manner: and so he propounded his wave-theory as a literal truth.

But immediately he came up against a difficulty. All these other varieties of waves have one thing in common: they are all waves in a material medium. But light, we all know, can traverse a vacuum. If light be waves, he argued, it must be waves in *some* medium – some kind of transcendental matter, that exists even in a vacuum. Believing in the literal existence of light-waves, he was compelled to believe in the literal existence of this medium. Believing in the literal existence of the medium, he gave it a name – the ether. And he then very properly set to work to discover what he could about its nature.

Before long, he came up against some very curious difficulties. Apparently flawless arguments led him into contradictory positions. He was able to prove for instance that the ether must be one and the same everywhere: he was also able to prove that it must be absolutely without weight: while yet another argument showed conclusively that in the neighbourhood of any electron it must be far heavier than lead. Again, it was proved to be more fluid than the thinnest gas, and yet more rigid than steel. But the climax came with the famous Michelson-Morley experiment. For it was argued that if the ether was a fluid medium through which matter moved, it must be possible to measure the velocity of that ether-stream. A boatman does not take the same length of time to row half a mile across a river and back again as he does to row half a mile up the river and down again. If you know the speed at which he rows, the difference between the two times will enable you to calculate the strength of the current. A ray of light, in the same way, reflected across the ether-stream, should not take the same time to travel a given distance as a ray of light reflected parallel to the stream. So, by measuring the difference, it should be possible to measure the ether-flow. By most refined means, the experiment was performed; and it led to the astonishing result that there was no difference at all. There was *no* measurable ether-flow. It was therefore impossible to believe any longer in the literal existence of the ether as a medium of the waves of light.

It is idle to speculate on the nature of the ether. A shepherd's crook is made of wood: but not even the maddest theologian would speculate as to what kind of wood the Good Shepherd's crook is made of. The story of the Good Shepherd is a parable: the wave theory of light is likewise a parable. Grasp that, and the rest will come easily. For after the wave-theory came the quantum-theory. Light, it was found, did not in all respects even mathematically act as a wave: in certain respects it acted like a shower of particles. For instance: the wave-theory cannot wholly account for such a phenomenon as the taking of a photograph. Each minute particle on the sensitised plate can only be either white or black. There is no such thing as greyness of an individual particle: the tone of any given patch on a photograph is due to the close or sparse grouping of pure black and pure white particles. But all particles are equally sensitive. Why when the shutter is opened are some particles black-ened, then, and others left white? Does this not look as if the plate were being bombarded with a shower of bullets, rather than as if it were struck by a homogeneous wave? Here is an analogy. As I speak to you now, waves of sound carry my voice down the hall. By the time my voice reaches the back rows, it is weaker than when it reaches the front rows: but it is still continuous. It does not leave anybody out. Now suppose that instead of being a lecturer, I am a dictator. Instead of trying to convince you with my voice, I try to convince you with a machine-gun. The effect will be very different. The rain of bullets will spread out. Those who are hit will equally be killed, whether they are in the front rows or in the back. The difference is that more of you in the front rows would be killed than at the back. At the back, the trajectories will be more widely separated.

And that, gentlemen, in spite of the wave-theory of light, is what seems to happen when we take a photograph. But how can the same thing be both a wave and a shower of separate particles? True. But how can mankind be both a flock of sheep, and at the same time a field where a Sower went forth to sow? Both are parables, and must be understood as such. The scientist, when he uses words to say the unsayable, and the poet, when he too uses words to say the unsayable, must equally use a translogical association of ideas.

So we see that in verbal expression at least they meet on common ground.

I said earlier that two courses were open to the scientist. When verbal language ceased to be able to express his meaning literally, there still remained another language, the language of mathematical symbol: and this language continued to be adequate (or rather, could be adapted and made adequate) to describe literally what might be beyond common sense. This adaptability may appear at first rather surprising, for have we not seen that it is some of the apparent truths of mathematics which break down first when it is attempted to carry them from the realm of the middle-size to the realm of the very large or the very small? We saw, for instance, that the three angles of a triangle ceased to add up to two right angles, if the triangle was sufficiently large. At this point surely the mathematician and the scientist would find themselves at loggerheads. Yet they do not; and the reason must be examined rather carefully, for it is of the utmost importance. The reason that mathematics could be adapted to describe the truths of the physical world is, paradoxically enough, because mathematics has no basis in the data of the physical world at all. It did not in the least embarrass the mathematician to be told that experiment in the physical world showed that in certain cases the laws he had formulated about triangles did not apply: because he knew that in the physical world there is no such thing as a triangle. None of the elements of geometry are to be found in the physical world. To begin with, there is no such physical thing as a point. A point is defined as being infinitely small, but having position: but the smallest known component of matter is not infinitely small, and has no definable position. Likewise there is, in the physical world, no such thing as a line, and no such thing as a plane. When, therefore, the mathematician defines some basic geometric concept, such as a point, his definition is not a description of something which he has observed. What he says in effect is this: *if* such a thing as I now define existed, certain arguments would logically follow. Geometry is abstract logic, in which the premises are not observed but invented. Now see what follows. Euclidian geometry is based on the assumption of three dimensions. But that is a purely fortuitous assumption. It makes no statement about the physical world. And so it does not embarrass the mathematician in the least to be asked to devise a different geometry of four dimensions (as it embarrasses some of us to be asked to believe in a world of four dimensions.) The geometrician, the pure geometrician that is to say, is willing to devise you a geometry in as many dimensions as you like; or even a geometry of no dimensions.

That is why the scientist found mathematics a language able to describe for him all that he discovered, because it was a language infinitely adaptable. It could be adapted to the new, just because it had no roots in the old. But let us not forget this. It has *no* roots in the new either. Mathematical truth no more depends upon the truth of the new physics, than it depended upon the truth of the old physics. Actually, of course, the truth of the mathematician and the truth of the physicist are wholly different in kind. Their systems are diametrically opposed. The truth of science is proved by experiment: the truth of mathematics can never be proved by experiment. The rigour of mathematical law is absolute: the rigour of scientific law, contrary to the belief of the man-in-the-street, is mostly relative and calculable. If it were possible to imagine a single exception to a mathematical law, that law would be automatically invalid. But this is not at all the case of the majority of natural laws: they are not such iron and necessary things, that their breaking is beyond the conception of man or God. They are laws of Chance, rather than laws of Certainty. It is not logically inconceivable that they can be broken: it is only very unlikely that it will happen. Toss a penny four or five times and you will not be unduly surprised if it turns up heads every time. Toss it ten thousand times, and you would be very surprised indeed if that happened. Indeed the likelihood of any natural law being broken is generally inversely proportional to the number of individual items concerned. It is because most natural laws refer to an enormous aggregate of individual items: the millions of molecules, for instance, in a single drop of water: that we put the chance of their being broken beyond the realm of probability. It is not unlikely that one of my audience may have a fit during the next five minutes, and have to be carried out: ambulance brigades are organised for just such a possibility. It is unlikely that six of my audience will be seized with apoplexy at the same time. It is very unlikely that the entire audience in the course of the next five minutes will be stricken with apoplexy, and my address thus come to an untimely end. It is very unlikely, but it is not inconceivable. In the same way it is not inconceivable that a deflated motor-tyre owing to an extraordinary chance commotion among all the molecules concerned, might pump itself up: but the numbers concerned are so large, that it is so unlikely, that anyone who waited for it to happen rather than fetch a pump would be rather foolish. That is all we mean when we say that such a happening is against the laws of Nature. It *is* inconceivable, on the other hand, that any one of the Sequences of Natural Numbers should disobey the general rules which govern the rest. Mathematics, which gave the Laws of Chance to Science, does not bow her own head to those laws. Mathematics is sometimes described as the science of number. No description could be more misleading, for no two systems of thought could be more diametrically opposed than science and mathematics.

We thus see how an extraordinary confusion of thought on a matter of the primest philosophical interest has come into being: a confusion which has infected, I am afraid, even some of the greatest of our physicists. They have adapted and adopted mathematics to be the language in which they describe their scientific discoveries. They forget that in so doing they have both adapted and adopted it, and they begin to believe that mathematics is the *natural* language in which to describe the universe. No pure mathematician could make such a mistake, knowing as he does that the basic concepts of mathematics are not found in the natural world, but are logical assumptions. He knows that he only takes out of an enquiry what he puts into it. The scientist forgets it. Science approaches experience with the technique of numbers: it divides the continuum into aggregates and classes. As the enquiry progresses, as the scientist gets further from his starting-point, and

apparently nearer to his solution, bit by bit everything slips through his
net, but that conception of number with which he started out. He looks
in the structure of the electron, in the shape of the universe, in the
nature of time for some kind of absolute reality, and what does he find,
or at least what up till now has he found? Six numerical constants,
which it seems impossible to reduce further: Planck's constant, which
determines the size of the quantum, and the degree of uncertainty in the
position of an electron; c, which for want of a better description we call
the velocity of light, though there are difficulties in considering it a
velocity at all; the gravitational constant; the charge of an electron; the
mass of an electron; and the mass of a proton. He finds at the end of his
search – numbers. And forgetting number was the very thing he
himself brought to the search, he is tempted to conclude that there is an
absolute and mystical reality in number.

This is only anthropomorphism in a refined form. When man first
studied nature, he conceived it in his own image. The lightning struck
him because he had offended it. Tempestuous seas were angry: the sun
ripened his crops out of kindness of heart. Bit by bit, he has shredded
away one clinging anthropomorphic conception after another. But
Science, being human enquiry, cannot hear any answer unless it is
somehow couched in human tones. The nineteenth century still
thought of the stars in their courses as obeying laws, like any human
population. The twentieth century advanced further: but even to-day,
as we can see, ineradicable anthropomorphism remains. For God, it
seems, is now the Great Mathematician. He no longer reveals Himself
as an angry God in the hurricane, or a benign God in the warmth of
summer, but He reveals Himself as a calculating God in h, and c, and e,
and π.

Primitive man stood among the mountains and shouted aloud
against a cliff. Echo brought back his voice, and he believed in a
disembodied spirit. To-day, the scientist stands counting out loud in the
face of the unknown. Numbers come back to him and he believes in the
Great Mathematician.

You will remember the analogy I used when I spoke of the
astronomer projecting, with his micrometer eye-piece, a fine net-work
of lines on to the continuum of the sky. I have tried to show number as
the net-work which the scientist, filled with an inward compulsion to
apprehend and to describe, projects for the purpose upon the
continuum of experience. Moreover I think now we have reached a
stage where it is possible to define, to mark the limits, of scientific

enquiry. For if we imagine that the whole of the perceived is the subject-matter of science, and all truth its goal, we make a grave mistake. Number is the method of science; then scientific enquiry is limited by its method. It only believes what can be observed: yes, but it is not (and by its nature it cannot be) concerned with all that can be observed. Science is only concerned with what is numerable. The scientist cannot consider an object in itself: he can only consider it as one of a group of objects, and he can only consider in it those qualities which are common to the group. He is not concerned with individuals, but (as the whole character of the laws he formulates reveals) with aggregates.

The scientist would have you define him as one who only believes what can be observed. But this definition is wholly inadequate. It applies rather to the poet. It applies equally to the truly religious man: he too only believes what he observes. No, the phrase which more truly limits and defines scientific enquiry is this: *whatever is not numerable is irrelevant to science.*

With the numerable for his subject matter: with numbers for the tools of his enquiry: need we feel any very great awe, or mystical satisfaction, or surprise, if six numerical constants are the Ultimate Truth he finds?

The poet too is moved by an inward compulsion to apprehend, and to communicate what he apprehends. He too only believes what can be observed. He too, like the physicist, expresses his meaning largely by a translogical association of mental images. But there the likeness ends. The net-work he projects upon the continuum is different. For he neither divides the continuum, nor regards its points as members of an aggregate. He is concerned, with an infinitely sensitive technique, in the expression of the relationship between parts that are not discrete.

I should have liked, if there were time, to have attempted the same kind of analysis of the poet's net-work, which I have attempted of the scientist's net-work and of the mathematician's: (or rather of the endless variety of his net-works). But the subject is too complex to tackle shortly, and is better left alone than botched. To attempt it would more than double the time for which I have already trespassed on your attention. For poetry is not, like science, or mathematics, a given object, the nature of which one can determine by examination. Poetry is a word which we all have the right to apply as we like. When a chemist is given a certain white powder and told to analyse it, there can be only one true answer. Other answers may be plausible, but they cannot be right. On the other hand, when the poet or critic is set down to say what he thinks poetry is, almost all answers, whether plausible or not, can be right. There is no such thing as a wrong theory of poetry – except a theory which precludes the truth of other theories. Just as the indefiniteness of the position of an electron is one of the few definite things we know about the electron, so the infinite diversity of the essence of poetry is the only single thing we know about that. Poetry is not a given white powder on which we are asked to stick the correct label. The word poetry rather is a label which we are given, and which we are invited to stick upon what we will; for poetry is a name which different generations and different people have used to describe absolutely different things; and no one has any right, I maintain, to say "now at last we have found the final white powder to which alone this label may be stuck".

What then may be concluded? More than anything it is the claim to catholicity of investigation, and monopoly of truth, on the part of science, which so irritates the minds of many poets that they will have nothing to do with it. Remove that claim to monopoly, and I think the poet and scientist will be better bed-fellows in future. Let the physicist, like the poet, watch his own mind working, and let him not mistake its shadow for the outline of God.

And for the poet, what is the conclusion? Your calling (which you are probably as ready as I am to leave without a definition), you know to have a true inner validity: and you see that even science can have no more. Therefore, let the net-work you project on experience be the unhampered cast of your own mind, and no other. Remember that the task you have undertaken is too great to accomplish only by taking thought. It is the blind giant under your mind who must grasp at the pillars between which he stands. Therefore learn what you can about your own technique, not in order to practise the devices which you discover, but to abandon them: for in poetry practice makes imperfect. Therefore do not in a slack way write loosely about what is merely under your nose: wait till in a fiery way you have to write what is under your mind. In short, if you can escape the necessity, do not write or paint at all: for it is only if you cannot help it that there is any possibility of its being worth doing: and even then the possibility, God forgive us all, is rather remote.

The Voice and the Pen

Some say that Man's kingdom over the beasts is coming to an end. They say the human race is destroying itself by that very cleverness which gave it supremacy.

Well, consider for a minute *how* Man became the King of Beasts. Was it entirely his cleverness? Do you know, I am not so sure. Consider first things first, and note, first that man is *physically* superior to other beasts. Naturally I don't mean that he is superior in every physical aptitude to every beast; but he is an all-rounder, he is more adaptable. He lives longer. He can stand greater extremes of climate. He is less specialised than most other species. He can't swim better than a fish or climb better than a monkey, that is true: but he can swim better than a monkey and climb better than a fish. And he is a remarkable stayer. In a race from London to York a man can beat a horse. Again, I have seen a man swim round a pool after a salmon till he tired it out. At last he caught and landed the fish with his bare hands.

However, this general physical superiority is not the whole story. Man has developed two particular physical organs in a way no other beast at present can rival. He can use his hands and he can use his tongue, incomparably. His hands help him to make and use tools: whereas few beasts can use tools, and only most exceptional beasts can make them. But above all, with his tongue he can talk.

Now it is the power to talk, even more than the power to use tools, which gave man the lead: because talking means teaching. Whatever new thing is conceived by one man can be taught to other men: imperfectly perhaps, but much more efficiently than by mere imitation, which is the only way animals can learn from each other. Imitation can only teach actions: it takes language to teach thinking.

It is a moot point whether animals think, though generally it is at least conceded that very few of them do much thinking. But perhaps it is worth considering whether a much larger proportion of *men* would think, off their own bat, if the words of others had not constantly been exciting the dormant faculty in them, from childhood.

But even speech, the spoken word, always had one drawback as a method of communication: teachers and taught must be in the same place at the same time. For this reason Humanity's progress must have been very slow before man called in his hands to help his tongue, and invented writing. For only writing can *bottle* knowledge and feeling, so that it can be transmitted across distances and down the ages. There has been a rapid acceleration in human progress in the last few thousand years. It is very doubtful whether there has been any commensurate improvement in the brain to account for it, even since the fairly early days of the human race. It would be far safer to put it down to the invention of the art of writing, which allows each generation to begin where the last left off.

If you doubt that argument, let me give a further illustration, where the invention is more recent. Just you *try* and do a difficult long division sum in Roman numerals! The fact is, of course, that until the Arabic system of numbering was invented, calculation (even what we should regard as simple calculation) was impossible. But without calculation there can be no advanced science. Now for various reasons the Arabic numerals were not finally adopted in Europe till the sixteenth century; and it is in the sixteenth century, accordingly, that modern science began that tremendous acceleration we see today. It is inconceivable to any biologist that in a few generations our brain should have changed so appreciably, that we should be born with an innate aptitude for science denied to Julius Ceasar and his contemporaries a mere sixty generations ago! It is just that the discovery of a system of numbering adapted to the needs of calculation at last provided science with an appropriate language.

Well, if literature, in the sense of stored-up communication, is of such supreme importance in the history of humanity, a few minutes spent in reflection upon certain aspects of its technique is not a waste of your time and mine. The points I want to make are few and simple; but it happens that they ought to be of particular interest to radio listeners.

Consider first the revolution wrought in literature by one mechanical invention, the printing press. Before the printing press was invented, the writer still reached the majority of his public not through their eyes but through their ears. Poetry was sung or recited, prose books too were recited or read aloud. I don't only mean heroic literature, such as Homer and *The Mabinogion*: it went on much later than that. Like music, today: music is for convenience written down as a score, but it is written to be performed, not to be silently conned. Or an architect's blue-prints. In the same way the writing down of literature for many centuries was simply a convenience, designed to *store communication*, and to ease its passage over space and time. It was, I say, a convenience, a means only: the ultimate act of communication still needed a mouth to speak and an ear to listen. For example, in Augustan Rome public recitation took the place of today's book publication: and the rich man in his library kept a slave to read his books aloud to him.

The slow and profound revolution brought about by the printing press, with its multiplication of copies, was the impetus it gave to the growth of the habit of silent, private reading. This change is of such importance that if I were asked to divide past written literature into two periods only, I should date the first period from the invention of letters, the second from the invention of the printing press and the habit of reading to oneself.

For the technical effect of this revolution, if slow, really *was* profound. You see it first in poetry, which acquired a subtler and quite different intricacy as words were no longer strung like beads, in one dimension, on a time-string, but laid out in a pattern which the eye could peruse almost in a single glance. Prose too developed a greater elaboration of structure, rolling out interminable periods gorgeous and majestic to the eye, which on the tongue would tax the lungs of an organ-bellows. Learned works could essay a greater complexity of learning, once the eye could turn back to recall a forgotten argument, could consult an index or a footnote.

But all this was not by any means pure gain. For one thing poetry, having ceased to be written in the mode of utterance aloud, had to be banished not only from the feast and the street corner, but from the theatre. The theatre has suffered from that ever since. Time was, that speech was nine-tenths of the play. Was it a bitter night? Then it was the dramatist's business to freeze your marrow with the words he put into the mouths of his shivering characters. Did the tramp of armies thunder on a dull and sodden countryside? Was there a tempest, and the ship sinking? Or did a roomful of itching unwashed noblemen simmer in the cookery of a Venetian summer? All this belonged once to the dramatist's art, not the producer's. Pasteboard scenery and coloured lights are a poor substitute for the Athenian or Elizabethan power, the poetic power, of evoking the living world in the course of dialogue. Pasteboard is infectious stuff, and soon spreads to the characters and the plot. Secondly, writing ceased to be concise. Once the reader became able to skip a boring passage and pick up the thread again later, the writer found he could allow himself boring passages with comparative impunity. If a bard or an orator was even temporarily boring, his audience left him altogether, and never came back! His exquisite peroration was uttered to the empty air – which made no recording.

Perhaps *because* the change was destined to be so profound, its action was exceedingly slow. The English Bible was written to be printed, but every word shows that it was intended to be read aloud. Even the nineteenth century had its Penny Readings, till they were killed by universal literacy and the cheap libraries. The home fireside had its family reading-aloud, so long as oil lamps left the greater part of the room in gloom: it was the general glare of electric light which killed *that* custom, actually in our own time.

Thus the last echoes of heard literature had only just died away when a second mechanical invention, broadcasting, set the pendulum swinging again in the opposite direction: a third period in the history of literature had begun.

The Voice had come back. But it is ironical that the invention of broadcasting should come *now,* at the time when contemporary writers are least equipped to make use of it. What a godsend it would have been to Vergil or Horace! How sonorously the amplifiers of the Surrey Side would have thundered the tones of Marlowe! Again, imagine yourself, as a contemporary of Bunyan, *hearing* in the solitude of your own chamber the still small voice of *Pilgrim's Progress* for the first time! Moreover what magnificent broadcasts Shakespeare would have written (if he were not too busy adapting Shaw's plays for the Talkies). But the silent writers of the twentieth century – the Voice was what they had just learned to do without altogether.

Some people think that radio will develop its own separate literature, that radio and the printed book will diverge further. I doubt that, genius is too rare: there is not enough literary talent to serve both, they must come together or one must starve. Some think that radio is the *only* literature of the future: that the present age of universal literacy is a passing phase, that reading and writing will become dead arts because, what with telephones and dictaphones and radio and talkies and all that, they will cease to be necessary in daily life. Like Greek and Latin. Frankly, I doubt that too. *I* believe they *will* come together, that there will be a remarriage of pen and voice: and I believe that literature will benefit. It may be good for little boys to be seen and not heard: but it is not good for books.

Liturgical Language Today

There was, once upon a time, an Act of Uniformity. Its chief object was that in every church throughout the country public worship should be couched in the same words and the same acts. A traveller from Northumberland should be able to walk into a church in Truro, any Sunday morning, and hear the same words spoken or sung and see the same things done as in Newcastle-on-Tyne. That is the meaning of the title *The Book of* Common *Prayer;* the same words ascending from every church in the country, as uniform and indistinguishable as the smell of incense. Scattered in innumerable buildings, the whole Body of Christ should worship together in one single set form of speech.

Today that Act of Uniformity has become virtually a nothing. It is doubtful if there are any two churches in the whole country where, throughout, exactly the same things are said and done today; any single church anywhere in which the text and rubrics of the legal Book of Common Prayer are followed nowadays without one jot or tittle of alteration. Maybe the whole Body of Christ – or rather, that part of it we call the Anglican Communion – maybe it still prays together in harmony; but it certainly does not pray together in unison.

We tend no longer even to call it the *Book of Common Prayer;* more fashionably we call it the ''1662 Book'' – just one form of prayer out of many. Indeed the Overseas Provinces have long ago for the most part openly abandoned it: they have drawn up their own new national Books of Common Prayer.

Thus it is unrealistic to talk of our liturgical reformers as men setting out to demolish any solid standing edifice to replace it with a new one more up-to-date and more to their taste. The edifice is already crumbling irretrievably in effect. In effect, it is today little more than a beautiful ruin. The question before us is not whether we are to have a new Book of Common Prayer, but rather whether we are to have a book of *common* prayer at all.

However, is any set form of prayer desirable? Impromptu prayer, say some, is so much more spontaneous. But the insurmountable difficulty with all impromptu public prayers is that they have to be prayed by the Minister alone – even if the congregation endorses them with a final "Amen". Only if the congregation knows already what the minister is going to say can the congregation ever truly accompany, rather than follow, his praying.

Again, is it still possible? Is the whole concept of public worship – and indeed, private worship too – a properly Christian practice these days? There are theologians who doubt it. A century ago F.D. Maurice said: "Religion against God. This is the heresy of our age." Today, Pastor Bonhoeffer's *Letters and Papers form Prison* – smuggled out of the concentration camp before Hitler finally hanged him – are being more read than ever; and Bonhoeffer certainly seems to expect a day when Christianity will discard altogether the entire concept of 'religion' as a worn-out coat, a mere passing phase in the Coming of the Kingdom. Bonhoeffer argues that God Himself is teaching us now to do without Him. He asks "What place remains for worship and prayer in an entire absence of religion?" *Homo religiosus* is becoming extinct, and Bonhoeffer calls those who still envisage Christianity in terms of religion a 'dubious group', survivals unhappily born out of time: just as Don Quixote was an unhappy anachronism born outside the Age of Chivalry.

But this is a hard saying, this about a totally religionless Christianity: and I don't pretend to more than a glimmering understanding; for surely one has to be as deeply and totally God-given a man as Bonhoeffer himself before one can think adequately in Bonhoeffer's terms.

At any rate, I think we *homines religiosi* still exist in considerable numbers among Christians – we Don Quixotes; and we are going to go on needing our common forms of prayer and Eucharist for some time to come. That, after all, is the assumption on which this school has been convened.

We are assembled this week to discuss liturgical reform. But today we limit ourselves to one particular aspect of it – liturgical language. This morning all overtly theological questions are taboo for the simple and obvious and unanswerable reason that I am not a competent person to involve in them. All the same, this taboo lands us in a dichotomy which is wholly unnatural; for liturgical speaking cannot really be separated from theological thinking.

Language is thought, inseparable from thought. No scalpel can separate it from thought without leaving a bleeding mess. We cannot speak without thinking (unless we are parrots or tape-recorders). We cannot think without at least inwardly speaking – unless we are painters, inventors, musicians (or perhaps, lovers). You cannot skim off language like a membrane from the surface of your thought, any more than you can detach the visible glittering part of an iceberg from its dumb submerged bulk. Like the visible part of the iceberg, language (together with such non-verbal communications as a smile or a kick-in-the-pants) is merely that small but integral part of our thinking which shows above the surface: which is at least dimly discernible by other people.

If then, liturgical language is truly inseparable from theology, there is only one way in which we can usefully discuss language in apparent separation: that is, where we can relate it to a theology which is 'given', an already-formulated liturgical theology. So I propose to spend most of the time allotted us this morning in taking a brief look at the language of the 1662 Book, since there for us the theology is 'given' and familiar; we shall then try to separate off from the untouchable theological difficulties that contribution which purely semantic difficulties have made to the crumbling of the edifice of our Common Prayer today.

In this way, at least by inference, we may perhaps learn something of value towards the construction of edifices yet to be built.

Some of you, I know, feel that certain theological emphases in that three-hundred-year-old Book have proved ephemeral, a flogging of dead controversies: the growing-pains of the young Anglican Church rather than its abiding content: or downright un-Christian, even. Thus they feel called on to distinguish (in the words of Canon Pawley) "the promptings of the Holy Spirit in 1662 from the sinful resistances of contentious men". Now, maybe these *are* indeed the difficulties which chiefly bedevil the intelligent parish priest these days, the difficulties which have set him tinkering personally with the structure as he does almost everywhere tinker. But I don't think those are the principal difficulties which today bedevil the layman, even the intelligent layman: for the simple reason that they are imperceptible to him because the language of the 1662 Book is something which he no longer understands when he hears, and which therefore he is unable to mean when he says (however much he loves and admires it and reacts emotionally to it). The 1662 Book today is no more couched in "language understanded of the people" than were, three or four hundred years ago, the Latin Missal, Breviary, Manual and Pontifical which the successive Books of Common Prayer replaced. The layman nowadays understands scarcely one single thing he hears or says in church.

Both above and below the chancel steps there is a very strong unwillingness to recognise this. Below the steps, the language of our weekly services, in all its dignity and beauty and sonorous rhythm, has become so familiar and so endeared to the faithful layman that it scarcely enters his head he is not understanding what he hears, and so, not meaning what he says. Among the clergy there is an even greater unwillingness. Because *they* understand the services they conduct, it is difficult for them to realise that the ordinary layman half the time hasn't the foggiest idea what it is all about.

If the clergy consider the semantic problem at all, it is usually to assume that the sole difficulty inherent in Prayer Book language is its sometimes antiquated vocabulary. If this were indeed the crux, all that would be needed would be a little simple instruction, and the occasional use of a blue pencil. It would have to be explained to congregations, for example, that "Prevent us, O Lord, in all our doings" does *not* mean "Go and see what little Tommy is doing and tell him not to": and we must change certain phrases – we must turn "bishops and curates" into "bishops and parish clergy". And so on, and so on.

Now it is true that careful instruction could do a lot to make congregations understand the services better. Personally, I would like to see far more Sunday pulpit-time given to explaining that service of which the sermon is (or should be) an integral part: less to a general moralising which so often seems to have so little discernible connection with its immediate liturgical context. But the real difficulty goes far deeper than occasional difficulties of vocabulary. It lies in the prayer-book employment of a syntax entirely alien to modern English speech. *Syntax* is the crux.

For syntax is the structural frame of thinking; and please remember that we laymen simply cannot think in a frame entirely alien to our habitual thinking, however familiar the vocabulary, or however well we have learned the special meanings of the words out of which that frame has been built.

I take it that by now most of us have seen a Shakespeare play acted in modern dress; a cocktail-drinking Hamlet, and a Polonius shot with an automatic. I wonder if your reaction was the same as mine? For to me, instead of bringing Shakespeare up to date, this seemed rather to emphasise the distance between his age and ours. It brought into relief the completely different cast of thought of our own age and one which took six lines of blank verse to say "Have a drink, old man!" Now, semantically the 1662 Book is far more remote from us than are the plays of Shakespeare. Those plays, after all, were originally composed in English. They were thought in English, by an Englishman. But so much of the *Book of Common Prayer* was not: it was thought in Latin. Moreover it was thought in Latin many centuries before 1622, before 1549; and has been only half-translated into the English language – even into the normal English of 1549-1662. I say 'half-translated' because the Latin sentence-structures have been so often retained.

Now I think, too, this latinate sentence-structure is the very reason why the layman's difficulties go so largely unrecognised by the majority of clergy. They, the majority of our clergy, unlike the majority of their congregations, have still had classical educations. Right back in their school-days, before the skeletal frames of their minds had become rigid and set, they have in some measure been taught to think as the Romans once thought and to pour the fluid of their pliable young thinking into the elaborate mould of the Ciceronian sentence. They have learned to do this so early that now they can at will and almost unconsciously switch their thinking to the requirements of Latin thought. The ease with which they do this makes them unable to realise how impossible it is even for the most intelligent layman to do the same if he has not had a classical education: if perhaps he is even unfamiliar with any other language-structure than that of his own English language.

Why, even the sort of sentences I am using in addressing you now – how easy would you find them to follow if you had not had a classical education? Or at least, if you were not already familiar with the semi-latinate English which we who have had classical educations tend willy-nilly to use on public occasions? But the thinking of the ordinary modern Englishman, however intelligent, is normally couched more in the sentence-structure of the *Daily Mirror* than of Cicero. How on earth, then, is he to learn to think in the involved and elongated sentences of so much of the *Book of Common Prayer!* – Prayers where the rare fullstop is more a concession to the limited capacities of even clerical lungs than a genuine pause in the argument.

Now make no mistake: I am not suggesting that a reformed liturgy should use the vocabulary of the *Daily Mirror* any more than it should utter the thoughts of the *Daily Mirror*. Nor am I making Ruskinian proposals that we should try to weed *words* of latin origin out of our vocabulary – calling an 'omnibus' a 'folk-wain', and suchlike nonsense. What I do assert is that the modern Englishman normally thinks in short sentences almost bereft of subordinate clauses and parentheses. Again, he leaves the relation between these sentences to be implied by their mere juxtaposition without any of the explanatory conjunctions so beloved of the latinist (he leaves a spark-gap for the meaning to leap, rather than a connecting wire to conduct it). He certainly does not think in these immense periods punctuated by rare full-stops: why, it would be truer to say that he thinks in a series of full-stops punctuated by rare words.

Even the language of the Authorised Version of the New Testament (at any rate, the Gospels and Acts) is more comprehensible to the modern Englishman than the language of the Prayer Book. This is because it is a translation not from Latin but from Greek, and the thought-structure of New Testament Greek is nearer akin than Latin is to modern English. All the same, it has been thought necessary to re-translate the New Testament into modern English. How much more necessary, then, it is, to re-translate the *Book of Common Prayer,* even if we have no intention of changing its theological content.

Indeed, I only see one alternative. If the old wording is to be retained (I am speaking of public worship, of course, not private Daily Offices), then we shall be forced to do as the R.C.'s do and issue to the faithful an explanatory running commentary. This they can study and keep by them in their pews, and so get some inkling of what is going on so unintelligibly around them. I see no third way out.

Take for an example that 'Exhortation' which precedes the General Confession both in Morning and Evening Prayer (but which is seldom delivered in full these days). In its syntactical construction surely this is one of the most involved and difficult pieces of liturgical writing in the whole book; and it is indeed unfortunate that this obstacle to the understanding should come at the very beginning of our services. How many among your congregation, do you think, even in a lifetime of church-going, have successfully disentangled the two main threads of its argument, which start separately and then are brought together half way through? How many of them realise that the preceding 'sentences' are in fact an integral part of the exhortation itself? Indeed, how many ministers read these sentences as such – as being actual examples of those "sundry places" in which the Scripture moveth us to confession?

Yet in paraphrase the meaning can be made quite clear. After reading two or three of the given penitential texts, the minister goes on to say in effect:

These sentences are only a few of the places where the Bible tells us to admit to ourselves our sinfulness, and to confess it humbly and sadly to God without trying to make ourselves out any better than we are, and to ask Him to forgive us. We should do this all the time and wherever we may be. But especially should we do it here and now; for now we have come together to thank Him, to praise Him, to listen to Him, and to pray to Him – laying before Him our spiritual and our bodily needs as well. First, then, come with me before the throne of God, all of you, and with pure hearts and humble voices join me in saying:

Then follows the General Confession.

This exhortation to confession, then, is much more than an exhortation to confession. The pith of it rather is its statement of the four reasons why we are assembled, the four things we have come to church to do. But we ought to *begin* by confessing our sinfulness and asking God's forgiveness; for only so can we now or ever put ourselves into a fit state to do what we have come together to do – that is, thank God, praise Him, listen to Him and pray to Him.

How many among your congregation, I repeat, have any idea that this simple meaning is what it is all about? Alas, I think most people simply regard it as a sort of preliminary incantation, a meaningless recitative by which the parson warms up his engine before launching into the real business to follow.

Now the meaning of a paraphrase like that may be clear as glass at the very first reading and yet the language not be a perfect example of all that liturgical language should be. After all, the meaning of the *Daily Mirror* is usually as clear as glass; but nobody wants to read his *Daily Mirror* twice. Liturgical language has to be read many more times than twice. For language to be eligible for frequent reading with profit it must have further depths and ramifications of meaning to reveal, bit-by-bit, to the frequent reader (this is where, for example, the lyrics of Herrick differ from the *Daily Mirror*).

You know those boxes of picture-blocks that children play with? When each block is set in the right place and the right-way-up and the right-way-round they make a complete picture of (say) a jet aeroplane. But then you carefully turn the whole box upside down; and behold, there is a complete picture of a puppy drinking from a bowl. Then you roll each row of blocks over on its side; and here is yet another picture – of a lion fighting with a bear, perhaps, or the Tower of London at sunset. In fact there are as many pictures as the blocks have sides. Now great English poetry is like that; and so should English liturgy be. In fact, this multiplicity of meaning revealed when we roll whole contexts of words over on their sides in our minds is the peculiar genius of the English language. Most other European languages – especially Latin ones – pride themselves that in their perfection they say one thing only and say it unequivocally: the one thing which the poet has in his mind to say – they mean that, and they can mean nothing else. But writing in English has a different kind of perfection. A consummate English poem means *all* the things which the poet has in his mind to say – all these things at once, however diverse. Those examiners are wrong who ask the student whether a passage means A, or B, or C, when the proper answer is that it means A and B and C all together. English liturgical writing in its perfection should do the same. However clear and limpid at first reading the top-meaning, there should be no end to the under-meanings which time and study will uncover. That is the only true dignity of language and the only true vigour of language: without it, conscious archaisms give only a sham dignity, and the 'vigour' of conscious colloquialisms is equally sham.

This fusion of many meanings into a single context is like the bond of marriage: two meanings cleaving together till they become one Word.

Then again, as well as this simultaneity of meanings there is a progression of meanings – and that progression of meanings has as well its own meaning too. A number of notes are played together in a chord of music, but also there is a progression of the chords one after the other. So, as each word is uttered one after the other, these meanings follow each other, and play in-and-out of each other, and weave their tracks into each others' tracks like a school of dolphins dancing round the prow of a ship. But (again as in music) there has to be a precise timing, a split-second timing of the impact of every one of these meanings on the ear and on the mind. That calls for a recognisable rhythm. For rhythm is the time-frame which prescribes the exact speed at which the several syllables leave the lips, just as the band-music predicts the exact instant of every foot-fall in a dance. Thus rhythm (and of course the euphonious placing together of all sounds – consonants even more importantly than vowels) is all-important in liturgy for two reasons. First and most obviously, because it carries the speaker along without tiring his voice and is equally welcome to the listening ear; but also for this second reason which I have just tried to explain; because it adds precise position in the fourth dimension (the dimension of *time*) to the merely Euclidian geometry of our static arrangement of meanings.

Writing recently in *The Bell,* the Bishop of Bangor remarked that little use seems to be being made of his permission for the Second Lesson in churches to be read from the New English Bible. I would like to suggest that one reason for this may be its inadequate rhythm and euphony. It seems to be written for the sittingroom rather than the lectern, in this respect. Again and again when preparing one's reading before going to church one is struck by how much more clearly the new translation brings out the sense of the passage, and so one decides to use it: then one stands up at the lectern and wishes one hadn't – simply because the language has not been sufficiently composed for reading aloud, as the older translations both in English and Welsh were both composed.

It is said that before the coming of printing the practice of silent mental reading was unknown: even if the reader was alone he read outloud in a low voice, or at least moved his lips (as children still do). After that, but before literacy became so common as now, most reading was still reading aloud: indeed illiteracy is surely one reason why in the 1662 Book so much is given to the minister to say (or the choir to sing) and so little to the congregation: most of them could not read. They repeated the General Confession *after* the minister, sentence by sentence: otherwise they were given only the simplest responses to learn by heart. Even before the coming of electric light, though most people knew how to read by then, much family reading still had perforce to be reading aloud because with a single paraffin lamp only one person in the room could properly see to read; and most writers bore this in mind, even fifty years ago. With the coming of electric light this last stronghold of reading aloud has vanished; and I wonder if perhaps we have lost the art of writing for it? I hope not (there is at least one modern invention which should give us reason to hope – the radio).

One thing at least is certain: if we cannot nowadays write for reading aloud, then there can be *no* liturgical language of today.

There is a story of the late Duke of Cambridge, about a hundred years ago. He was presiding over the Army Council, and they had been called together to decide the proper number of buttons to sew on a private's tunic. I say 'presiding', but he slept soundly throughout (according to the story). However they had to wake him at last to give his chairman's casting vote, and he didn't even know what they had been discussing. But that made no difference: "You may depend upon it, gentlemen", said the Duke with deep conviction, *"any change will be for the worse"*.

Just possibly that guiding principle of the good Duke's has governed too long our attitude to liturgical reform – and more particularly, to the reform of liturgical language. When Cyril and Methodius first ventured to translate the Latin liturgy into the Slav tongue there were 9th-century clerics who argued that the only permissible languages for divine worship were Latin, Hebrew and Greek, because those three were the only languages chosen by Pontius Pilate for the superscription of the Cross. It is all very well today to smile at the naivety of such an argument from the liturgical authority of Pontius Pilate: but are 20th-century clerics being all that more logical in nailing themselves to the language of a King Charles II?

The lovely language of the Prayer Book is, alas, no longer "understanded of the people". Our first need, then, is for short, simple, *English* sentences that say something clearly. But ease of comprehension at first hearing is only the beginning: what we say in our Common Prayer we repeat and repeat and repeat: if the words are to remain alive in our mouths after so much mouthing they must be able to reveal new facets of meaning every time we repeat them. Under their plain and simple appearance they must possess that compact multitudinousness of meaning which is the peculiar genius of the English tongue. Thirdly, liturgical language has to stand up to being delivered aloud without flagging as sound. It must be euphonious and rhythmical, with clear ringing consonants and rhythms which carry the voice along, and enhance it and swell it, and which point the progression of the meanings as they move.

New liturgy calls for bold linguistic experiment – bold, but skilled: as in the laboratory, where bungling slap-happy experiment leads only to a broken test-tube and a nasty smell. For liturgy is theology and poetry too. Divines are needed with all the theological meanings to be expressed in due proportion and relation at their finger-tips; but poets also are needed capable of crowding these meanings by the handful into every single pregnant word, till counting the meanings (in its context) of any word is like counting the angels on a needle-point ("in its context" mark you; for the true units of meaning are contexts, not isolated words). Again, no one would nowadays entrust new liturgy to one single theologian working entirely alone. Even the finest theologian has at least one bee in his bonnet: we want no *buzz* left aloud in our liturgy, so we give him the help and criticism of his peers. But similarly even the finest poet has his dull or vapid line, his over-idiosyncratic signature-tune: he too needs the help and criticism of his peers. A whole consortium of theologians which is also a nest of poets . . .

But even then (which could mean separately recruiting the skills necessary for both sides of the house) their work will go for nothing and will topple like a latter-day Tower of Babel in a dusty débris of dull bickering and committee-work and compromise unless it is inspired by the Holy Spirit. Only He from age to age can touch with His altar-coal human lips, teaching them even to lisp the due liturgical language of their day. It is not just a human skill.

Given at a Clergy School for the Dioceses of St. Asaph and Bangor in Summer 1962. Published in *Province* vol.XIII, no.4.

IV
Books and Authors

W.E. Henley

"I have no invention," Henley once said to a friend; and it is a curious confession for a poet to make – curious, but a very necessary remark for the critic to remember. We are so used to the poetry of invention – or poetry, at least, wherein fiction and figment (which is invention) plays an important part – that it is strange to have to admit that there can be poetry without it. One of the broadest of the innumerable definitions of art is "Truth tempered with falsehood": but it is unncessary to multiply demonstrations, where the single process of calling to mind any of that poetry one thinks great gives proof of the part invention has to play in it: the small germ of reality as it is known to the uninventive man. To add one other, and that one mathematical, to the pile of definitions, art might be called "Life *multiplied* by invention".

But such a definition, such a conception of art, will not go far to the understanding of the poetry of Henley, except in a few rare instances. Invention is largely the quality of a man who takes a natural delight in expression; but this is the poetry of a Herculean vigour of feeling struggling into expression pell-mell – willy-nilly – by sheer strength. Words seem never a pleasure to him, always something of a mystery: a delicate and incomprehensible barrier that he is tempted to tear up like the gates of Gaza. It is only in some of his later pieces that words acquire any significant meaning of their own, other than that of damnable hindrances to the expression of his feelings. Before he is an artist, he is a personality – a personality reaching expression *through* art in the sense that a man goes *through* a wall, not *through* a gate.

A great deal of his peculiarity is traceable to this very fact of personality, and to the events of his life. From his twelfth to his eighteenth year he was so crippled by tuberculosis that his life was in danger, and one foot was amputated, the other threatened; and it was only his courage in journeying to Edinburgh and putting himself under Lister's new antiseptic treatment that saved it. For eighteen months or so he was in hospital; and during those eighteen months he wrote what was

probably the first *vers libre* written in English by any of his generation –
the verses, 'In Hospital'. It was during this time that his friendship with
Stevenson began; he describes Stevenson in a sonnet as:

> Thin-legged, thin-chested, slight unspeakably,
> Neat-footed and weak-fingered: in his face
> Lean, large-boned, carved of beak, and touched with race,
> Bold-lipped, rich-tinted, mutable as the sea,
> The brown eyes radiant with vivacity –
> There shines a brilliant and romantic grace,
> A spirit intense and rare, with trace on trace
> Of passion and impudence and energy.
> Valiant in velvet, light in ragged luck,
> Most vain, most generous, sternly critical,
> Buffoon and poet, lover and sensualist,
> A deal of Ariel, just a streak of Puck,
> Much Antony, of Hamlet most of all,
> And something of the Shorter-Catechist.

Soon after leaving hospital he was appointed editor of the *London,* and
the major portion of his life was spent in controlling a series of
periodicals – all brilliantly edited, all publishing work since famous, all
tending in turn to the same financial crash: the *London,* the *Magazine of
Art,* the *National Observer,* and the *New Review* – after which he refused
to edit again. Throughout his life until 1898, when he was given a civil-
list pension, poverty dogged him; and disease and misfortune dogged
him always. He had only one child – Margaret – and in 1894 she
died.

This is a bare and jumbled summary of a tragic life, but sufficient,
perhaps, to give a certain background to the personal expression of his
poetry. Add to this that he had the physical build of a giant, and a
natural longing, like Stevenson, for a violent and outdoor life, which he
was never able to gratify.

"Desire makes verses," he wrote himself in his incendiary essay on
Burns, "and verses rather good than bad, as surely as fruition leaves
verses, whether good or bad, unmade." Poetry is often the sublimation
of two things – desire and sorrow. With desires he was plentifully
endowed by nature; with sorrow, by fortune. But besides his lack of
invention there is another lack: he was not a man of very shrewd or
particular observation. The poems 'In Hospital' recall – to those who
have such experiences to recall – what they have themselves seen and

felt, without adding much to the picture, or the experience. He does not seem to see more than the average patient, but he is more convinced of the importance of what he sees, more determined to remember and to communicate. He is, in fact, rather an exaggeration of the ordinary man than a man actually distinct from his fellows.

This may sound harsh – impudent – this belittling of a dead lion; for lion he was. But his great merits are the merits of personality rather than of art – integrity, generosity, courage, and a sufficiency of erudition. All who first emerged to the light of publicity by his help bear equal witness to these qualities; as an editor he was almost unsurpassable. Was he no artist at all, the utterance of such a man could not be insignificant; and at times, most emphatically, he is an artist: at times the breadth of his genius was forced and compressed through the Straight Gate of expression.

"The greatest poetry," said recently one of 'Henley's young men', now famous, "is statement. Its counterfeits are sentiment and rhetoric – rhetoric, the art of deceiving an audience; sentiment, the art of deceiving oneself." This rather disjointed preamble is intended to suggest that in looking for Henley at his finest we should pass over many of his most famous pieces (more especially the 'Verses in Time of War', 'England, my England', and the rest); pass over even the 'London Voluntaries', in spite of their intrinsic excellence; and turn, for instance, to his Epilogue to 'Rhymes and Rhythms', in which the superficial appearance of sentiment is belied by the real intensity of passion, too great for his besetting sin of exaggeration:

> These to you now, O, more than ever now –
> Now that the Ancient Enemy
> Has passed, and we, we two that are one, have seen
> A piece of perfect Life
> Turn to so ravishing a shape of Death,
> The Arch-Discomforter might well have smiled
> In pity and pride,
> Even as he bore his lovely and innocent spoil
> From those home-kingdoms he left desolate!
>
> Poor windle-straws
> On the great, sullen, roaring pool of Time
> And Chance and Change, I know!
> But they are yours, as I am, till we attain
> That end for which we make, we two that are one:
> A little, exquisite ghost

> Between us, smiling with the serenest eyes
> Seen in this world, and calling, calling still
> In that clear voice whose infinite subtleties
> Of sweetness, thrilling back across the grave,
> Break the poor heart to hear:-
>   "Come, Dadsie, come!
> Mama, how long – how long?"

The 'Verses in Time of War' were written, not to deceive, but at least to persuade others; the 'London Voluntaries', though greatly superior to 'In Hospital', suggest, as they do, an exaggeration of the importance of feeling and observation itself not extraordinary. The difficulty of forming a judgment on Henley is great, because he does not fit into any ordinary scheme of the aesthetics of poetry as now conceived; he cannot be judged by beauty of form, by inter-relation of sound and image, the rhythmic order of ideas: these have small part in his conception. To judge him on his own ground, he must be judged by his feeling and passion; by its sincerity and its intensity. Moreover, one must remember that he was born in 1849, and lived in an age – as he himself put it – "under the shadow of the Albert Hat"; that his greatest periods of activity were the 'eighties and 'nineties – times still too close for the critic to set in perspective, but which abounded in sentiment and rhetoric; when the first duty of the artist was to shock; one can then realise the doubled sincerity of a man who shocked simply as an incidental to telling the truth, who struggled courageously with poverty and disease in an age when they were a morbid fashion among many who had but a bowing-acquaintance with either (so that what genius did not live in a garret at least pretended to it). There never was a man so free of pose as Henley, a more unconscious revolutionary.

Saturday Westminster Gazette,
19th March 1921.

John Skelton

Born *about* 1460   Died 1529

"Sic velut est Arabum phenix avis unica tantum
Terra Britanna suum genuit Skeltonida vatem."

It happens from time to time that some poet almost forgotten suddenly comes into his own. There is nothing strange and freakish about this: and it does not really give us license to crow over our fathers. The colour of the reading mind changes from one generation to another, as it changes from man to man: in becoming able to appreciate something our fathers found incomprehensible, or unpleasant, we generally lose our appreciation of something they found estimable. The ground shifts under us.

Certain poets have to wait a long time for the advent of a sympathetic generation: Skelton has had to wait four hundred years. Yet, you might say, in his own day his reputation was international: Oxford, Cambridge, and Louvain crowned him with laurel: he was tutor to Henry VIII and *Orator Regius:* Erasmus, Caxton, and other smaller fry praised him whole-heartedly: and he was a sufficiently popular figure for a whole cycle of myth to have accumulated about his personality. But the learned admired him for his learning, and the people admired him as one of the most amusing and boisterous writers of any century: Skelton, knowing himself to be not only a scholar and a jocular but a poet, looked to Posterity for nice appreciation. The quality of poetry in Skelton was one of which it was an impossibility absolute, in the rudimentary state of criticism and aesthetic theory, for the age of Henry VIII to have any inkling. (That they called him a poet, being deceived into a true verdict by irrelevancies, is nothing[1]). And so he placed his faith in Posterity: and Posterity has played the jade with him: never quite giving him his *congé*, she has kept him dangling after her through century after century – has been to him a sort of everlasting Fannie Brawne.

The reason for this neglect is simple and superficial. In the first place, he wrote at a time when the pronunciation of English was on the eve of a drastic change, and the dropping of the final *e* in so many words soon rendered his rhythms unintelligible. In the second, he came close before one of the greatest revolutions that ever transformed the surface of

literature – the Elizabethan Era. Precurring signs of that revolution
were already in the air: and he set his face against them. It is easy for us
now, prejudiced by a knowledge of what was to come, to blame him: it
is easy to explain after the race why such and such a horse won. But it
would have been impossible to guess, at that time, from the stilted
Italianate compositions of the opposite camp that the unaccountable
Spirit of the Lord would choose such dry bones for its dwelling. Judged
by themselves, they were worthless, and Skelton was right in con-
demning them. But he backed a loser: and has paid for his misfortune
with four centuries of neglect and incomprehension.

For four centuries he has lain in his grave, food for the grammarians.

Largely, they are to blame. If the critic is a man who has failed at one
of the arts, the scholar is generally a man who has failed at criticism. He
looks for no aesthetic worth in his subject-matter: for his purposes it is
irrelevant, hardly even an encumbrance[2]. If he made this position
clear, one would not blame him, one would not ask blood from a stone.
But he does not; he pretends to criticism for form's sake: he accepts
ready-made the judgement of the general, damning with one hand
what he edits with the other: he takes his judgement from the general,
while the general imagine that they are taking their judgement from
him. They respect him: he has read all these unheard-of people, he
knows: if there was any good in them, he would announce it. But he
does not announce it, because he could not see it, even if it were shown
him. God help any poet who hopes to be rescued from oblivion by the
scholars! His only hope is to be set some day before a sympathetic
generation in some form unencumbered by excess of learning, that his
readers may discover him for themselves. Even then, not till the very
servant-girls devour him by candle-light will it occur to his editors that
the subject of their life's work had any intrinsic value of its own.

Their treatment of Skelton has been particularly scurvy. Only one,
the Rev. Alexander Dyce, has taken him at all seriously. Such editions
as appeared before the time of Dyce were almost unintelligible
conglomerations of naïvely-accepted miscopyings. Dyce undertook the
great and necessary work of putting the text into an intelligible form:
and gave half his life to it. Dyce's edition is a fine piece of scholarship,
and the standard text on which all future work must be based. But it is
doubtful whether even Dyce realised the full aesthetic value of Skelton's
poetry. As for the others, they deserve all opprobrium. The writers of
literary histories have been content to repeat with parrot-like
persistence, one after the other, that Skelton was a witty but coarse

satirist, having occasionally a certain rude charm, but in the main bungling, disgusting, prolix, and tedious: and they have relegated him to that most damning of insignificancies, the part of an "influence". They have been content to leave Dyce's edition, published eighty years ago, not only unrevised, but out of print and now practically unobtainable. But, truly, Skelton is a poor satirst compared with his powers as a poet: his influence is negligible when compared with the value of his original work: and simply regarded as a rhythmical technician he is one of the most accomplished the language has ever known. There is more variety of rhythm in Skelton than in almost any other writer.

Take, for example, the first piece published in this book, 'Speke, Parot'[3]. They regard it as an unintelligible piece of political satire, interesting only for its references to Wolsey and the Introduction of Greek! Those last three stanzas, which set the pointer to the parable, which tell us that

> Parot is my owne dere harte . . .

– they are entirely overlooked. Yet no one who bears those three stanzas in mind can misread the rest, can fail to see the beauty of the whole conception. Shakespeare did not misread it: as his *Phoenix and Turtle* bears witness.

So much for the core of the poem. But alas!

> *Crescet in immensum me vivo Psittacus iste:*

Skelton, finding the Parot so convenient a mouthpiece for his views on things in general, has later hidden the sensitive mystery of his poem under a greal deal of additional matter that is simply concerned with mundane affairs. (For it is generally admitted that the poem, as it has reached us, is a hodge-podge composed at many different dates.) Admittedly it is a difficult poem: but the extraordinary sense of rhythm, the extraordinary intellectual grasp that not only makes every word significant but every juxtaposition of words, every possible turn and shade of meaning, render it one of those few poems that can be read with increasing admiration, increasing comprehension and delight year after year. The more one reads it, the more one learns of its meaning, the more certain one is of never getting to the bottom of it. It is a living thing, its roots branching innumerably: comprehension of it is interminable. And, as all fine poetry must, it baffles eulogy.

Far simpler, far more easily popular, is the 'Boke of Phyllyp Sparowe'. Here is no high lyrical mystery; only, in the words of Coleridge, "A beautiful and romantic poem": very simple and pathetic. Jane Scroupe, a school-girl of Carowe, mourns for her dead pet. It is remarkable that at a time when Elizabethan drama was still below the horizon Skelton should have so *characterised* the poem, have brought Jane so vividly into our minds, not by description but by the very words she speaks. In two things the mediaeval poets excelled, even the dullest of them – in the description of birds and young girls: Skelton, if in some senses he is the first of the Georgians, in another is the last of the mediaevals: he has brought these two things to a climax in 'Phyllyp Sparowe':

> It was so prety a fole,
> It wold syt on a stole,
> And lerned after my scole
> For to kepe his cut,
> With Phyllyp, kepe your cut!
>   It had a velvet cap,
> And wold syt on my lap,
> And seke after small wormes,
> And somtyme white bred crommes;
> And many tymes and ofte
> Betwene my brestes softe
> It wold lye and rest.

It is a pretty thing.

– Next, one is faced with

> The topsy-turvy tunnyng
> Of Mistress Elynour Rummyng.

The weak stomach will be turned by it: but those with a gizzard for strong meat will find it a remarkable piece. I do not speak of it as a precursor of the "realistic" school of poetry: it is more valuable than that. It is the processional manipulation of vivid impressions, the orchestration, the *mental* rhythm which strikes me. So far from calling it a realistic poem, I would call it one of the few really abstract poems in the language. Its aesthetic effect is that of a *good* cubist picture (or any picture dependent on form for its value).

It would be foolish to take each of his poems in turn: but one word should be said for the 'Garlande of Laurell'. "This," say the historians, "is the longest poem ever written by a poet in his own honour." They accuse the author of pomposity and vanity in consequence. I only ask you to read it: I do not think he makes any claims in it which are not justified: after all, he *is* the finest poet in England (Scotland is *hors concours*) between Chaucer and the Elizabethans, and he cannot be blamed for knowing it. If he errs, it is in attaching too much reverence to Gower and Lydgate, not to himself. Anyhow, the whole is very pleasant reading: and some of the incidental lyrics are wholly delightful.

What wonderful plays, one thinks after reading 'Phyllyp Sparowe,' he might have written: what easy characterisation! That he did write plays is known: and one, *Magnyfycence,* has survived. The others, like a great many of his poems, have unhappily vanished. The nineteenth century dubbed it "the dullest play in any language". From the point of view of the nineteenth century the judgment was admissible, seeing the ideal of drama it serves was not then invented: but not from the point of view of the twentieth. It is an abstract play, a sort of morality – still, even at the date I write, a little ahead of the times: but I believe that if the language were modernised and the whole produced with skilful expressionistic lighting it could not fail to create a sensation. Not in England, perhaps, for another twenty years or so: but I confidently recommend it to the notice of Berlin and Prague – and perhaps New York.

I have said very little about Skelton's life: very little is known. He was born about 1460, he made a brilliant reputation as a scholar, was tutor to Henry VIII, a notable figure at court and the friend of the Countess of Surrey. He became rector of Diss, in Norfolk. He was one of the broadest minded and yet most devoted of churchmen, and attacked vices within the church unmercifully. He was a bitter enemy of Wolsey – he, a country rector, was the only man in England who stood up to the Cardinal: and he died in Sanctuary at Westminster, where he had taken refuge from Wolsey's anger. Since marriage in a clergyman was an inconceivable crime, far worse than concubinage, he did not confess till on his deathbed that he regarded the mother of his children as his wife in the eyes of God: although he never made any secret of their relationship. The rest is myth, mostly apocryphal: but one passage from the *Merie Tales* I will quote, for there is something characteristic of the immense courage – intellectual and physical – of the man in it, whether it be true or not:

Skelton the next Sunday after went into the pulpit to preach, and said *"Vos estis, vos, estis, "*that is to say, You be, you be. "And what be you?" said Skelton, "I say, that you be a sort of knaves, yea, and a man might say worse than knaves: and why, I shall show you. You have complained of me to the bishop that I do keep a fair wench in my house . . . I *have* a fair wench, of which I have begotten a fair boy, as I do think, and as you all shall see. – Thou wife," said Skelton, "that hast my child, be not afraid; bring me hither my child to me!" The which was done. And he, showing his child naked to all the Parish, said: "How say you, neighbours all? Is not this child as fair as is the best of all yours? It hath nose, eyes, hands and feet, as well as any of yours: it is not like a pig, nor a calf, nor like no foul nor no monstrous beast. If I had," said Skelton, "brought forth this child without arms or legs, or that it were deformed, being a monstrous thing, I would never have blamed you to have complained to the bishop of me: but to complain without a cause, I say, as I said before in my antethem, *vos estis,* you be, and have been, and will and shall be Knaves, to complain of me without cause reasonable!"

Notes to Skelton

Notes.

1. "Who indeed as he obtained the Laurel Garland, so may I with good right yield him the title of a poet." – William Webbe, *A Discourse of Englishe Poetrie,* 1586.

   To be the *Poet Laureate* was to have obtained a certain University degree: and the word *poet* was often used as little more than a synonym for *scholar.* They had no conception of *poetry,* in the sense of the word meant nowadays. Perhaps *Maker* comes nearer to our use of the word *poet* than any other term in use in Skelton's age.

2. One gentleman, to whom the Editor was told to apply for information, answered that his interest in Skelton lay in the possibility of reconstructing the Church of Diss from the description of it in 'Ware the Hauke'. That was at any rate frank: the literary historians are not. See the *D.N.B.,* etc.

3. The sole reference to this poem in the *Dictionary of National Biography* is to say that it is "written in Chaucer's well-known stanza": which is not only inadequate, but also untrue. The rhyme-scheme is certainly that of Rhyme-royal: but the metre had never been used before; and so far as I am aware, has only been used once since – in 'Rocky Acres', by Robert Graves. I know of no other poem with more originality, more beauty, more subtle variety of rhythm than this same 'Speke, Parot'.

   But if I were to continue quoting the stupidities uttered about Skelton in high places, there would never be an end.

Introduction to *Poems by John Skelton,* (Heinemann, 1924).

Mrs Dalloway

To the poet the visible world exists: it shines with an intense brilliance, not only to the eye but to the touch, ear, smell, inward vision. (To the man-of-the-world, the visible world is unreal: his reality is a spiritual one: the only things which exist for him are his desires, and – in a lesser degree – his beliefs.) In Mrs. Woolf's new novel, *Mrs Dalloway,* the visible world exists with a brilliance, a luminous clarity. In particular, it is London: to the reader, London is made, for the first time (this will probably surprise him) to exist. It emerges, shining like crystal, out of the fog in which all the merely material universe is ordinarily enveloped in his mind: it emerges, and stays. The present writer has "known" London all his life: but Mrs. Woolf's evocation of it is of a very different quality from his own memories: a quality which answers the farmer's question, when he was puzzled as to why folk should pay five hundred guineas for a painting of his farm, when they could have the house itself for two hundred. To Mrs. Woolf London exists, and to Mrs. Woolf's readers anywhere and at any time London will exist with a reality it can never have for those who merely live there.

Vividness alone, of course, is not art: it is only the material of art. But Mrs. Woolf has, I think, a finer sense of form than any but the oldest living English novelist. As well as the power of brilliant evocation she has that creative faculty of form which differs from what is ordinarily called construction in the same way that life differs from mechanism: the same quality as Cézanne. In the case of the painter, of course, this "form" is purely visual; the synthesis – relation – rhythm – whatever you call it, is created on this side of the eye; while in the case of the poet the pattern is a mental one, created behind the eye of the reader, composed directly of mental processes, ideas, sensory evocation – not of external agents (not of the words used, I mean). So, in the case of Mrs. Woolf, and of the present novel, it is not by its vividness that her writing ultimately stays in the mind, but by the coherent and processional form which is composed of, and transcends, that vividness.

Philosophy as much as smell of violets is grist to the artist's mill: in actual practice it is generally more so. Here, Mrs. Woolf touches all the time the verge of the problem of reality: not directly, like Pirandello, but by implication. (She is not so prone to emphasis as Pirandello.) In contrast to the solidity of her visible world there rises throughout the book in a delicate crescendo *fear.* The most notable feature of contemporary thought is the wide recognition by the human mind of its own limitation; i.e., that it is itself not a microcosm (as men used to think) but the macrocosm: that it cannot "find out" anything about the universe because the terms both of question and answer are terms purely relative to itself: that even the key-words, *being* and *not-being*, bear no relation to anything except the mind which formulates them. (This is at least as old as Tao Tse, but until now has seldom been recognised by ordinary man.) In short, that logical and associative thinking do not differ in ultimate value – or even perhaps in kind. So, in this book each of the very different characters – Clarissa Dalloway herself, the slightly more speculative Peter, the Blakeian "lunatic", Septimus Warren Smith, each with their own more or less formulated hypothesis of the meaning of life – together are an unanswerable illustration of that bottomlessness on which all spiritual values are based. This is what I mean by fear.

To come to the matter of chronicle, this novel is an account of a single day in London life; its sole principal event is the return from India of Mrs Dalloway's rejected suitor; the other characters are in many cases not even acquainted with the principals – sometimes simply people they pass in the street, or even people who merely see the same aeroplane in the sky. Towards the end, one of these strangers flings himself from a window: and Mrs. Dalloway, after spending most of the morning wandering about Bond Street, gives a party in the evening. But then, Chronicle is an ass; this is an unusually coherent, lucid, and enthralling book, whatever he may suggest to the contrary.

Saturday Review of Literature,
16 May, 1925.

Seven Pillars of Wisdom

This week sixty thousand copies of *Seven Pillars of Wisdom* were let loose, and will very likely be sold. But not read. Many a thirty shillings will be a mere fee paid to fashion, or good intention, or hero-worship. For there are certainly not sixty thousand people alive in England today capable of reading the book. In length it runs well over a quarter of a million words: it is tightly packed: it is the expression of lofty, complex, and desperate mind.

By the same token, it will be reviewed at length in every paper. Many of the reviews will be by distinguished authors; by men who knew Lawrence, and on whom his impact was profound. Yet I doubt if any single review will be wholly satisfactory. The Turkish army could not contain the Arab revolt, because of the revolt's extension in depth. Likewise there is an extra dimension to this book, which must always remain oblique to the widest deployments of criticism.

Lawrence was more like an onion than an apple. You can peel an apple, and lay it bare. But it is not so easy, when peeling an onion, to know what skin to stop at. The really pertinacious can peel an onion until there is no onion – but that is a poor reward for their pains. Therefore mistrust people who say, "I knew Lawrence, he was so-and-so; beneath all his (what's-its-name) he was really (thingumabob)." Or rather, believe them, but remember that the skin they have found is no thicker than the one they have peeled off. The intense introspection of Lawrence was well aware of this. He knew that each skin was the actual product of the different layer beneath. He knew, for instance, that under his flight from publicity lay an appetite for glory; which itself overlay a contempt for all material achievement. Because he knew this, he wantonly added to his integuments outwards. If nothing else was at stake, the effect he chose to produce on any audience was generally the one he judged to be the hardest. Even a negative one. You often hear it said of some celebrity that you could feel his greatness the moment he entered a room. Therefore Lawrence went one better. He could be in a room without anyone noticing he was there, till he chose – a far harder achievement. This sounds as if he were only a kind of psychological conjuror, an adept at sleight-of-mind: a mountebank. There was that skin. But it was the thinnest of all. He was a great man, all right. For my own part, as a boy, I found in contact with Lawrence the highest kind of numinous excitement that I am capable of feeling.

Although this is the first public edition of the *Seven Pillars,* much of it has already been made public (in addition to Lawrence's own abridgement, *Revolt in the Desert*) by the two leading biographies, Graves and Liddell Hart. In Graves particularly, whole passages were incorporated, only transposed from the first to the third person. (In the circumstances this was wholly proper. Graves was writing at Lawrence's personal request, at high pressure, in order to forestall a "possibly inaccurate" Life by an author Lawrence detested.) But these abridgements do not at all detract from the value of the publication of the whole. Graves was concerned, in his abridgement, with extracting the narrative. As a true adventure-story, it can be compared with other true adventure-stories. Liddell Hart, was concerned with extracting the strategy. He ranks Lawrence, as a military artist, among the highest: and other military historians may argue the question in military terms. In both these spheres comparisons can be made, legitimately and easily; for neither of them contains the uniqueness of the book. (I must hasten to add that it does not lie, either, in its literary quality. Lawrence was not a natural poet. Brilliantly though he learned to write, his language remains, as it began, artificial: his medium is never more than the hand-maid of his meaning.) No, its uniqueness is spiritual. Here was a man of greater military ability (if we accept Liddell Hart) than Napoleon, prone at the same time to apply to meditation the same intense concentration that he applied to external problems. A man of the most burning activity, whose philosophy marched with the negative aspects of at least of the philosophy of Lao Tsu; and added to it a heightening, into incorporeal things, of the Islamic doctrine that to create is wicked. A leader who stripped himself, to the bare ego, of illusion; thus becoming an immense "capacity yawing rudderless"; and lent himself to further other men's purposes, to save, for others, the sin of creating from the sin of being botched creating; though fully conscious of the suicide his own integrity was thereby committing.

The central problem of the book, then, is the problem of excelling. It is implicit everywhere; but it is expressly discussed in two beautifully modulated chapters, the hundredth and the hundred and third. How can the man of greater capacity excel, without harming his neighbours? Are we "like cells of a bee-comb, of which one might change or swell itself, only at the expense of the whole"? Many would answer, No: for there lies the way of self-sacrifice, the way of the redeemer, the vicar. It was hardly to be expected that Lawrence would accept this at its face value:

> The self-immolated victim took for his own the rare gifts of sacrifice; and no pride and few pleasures in the world were so joyful, so rich as this choosing voluntarily another's evil to perfect the self. There was a hidden selfishness in it, as in all perfections. To each opportunity there could be only one vicar, and the snatching of it robbed the fellows of their due hurt. Their vicar rejoiced, while his brethren were wounded in their manhood. His purer part, for the mediator, might have been to stand

among the crowd, to watch another win the cleanness of a redeemer's
name. By the one road lay self-perfection, by the other self-immolation,
and a making perfect of the neighbour . . . To endure for another in
simplicity gave a sense of greatness. There was nothing loftier than a
cross, from which to contemplate the world. The pride and exhilaration
of it were beyond conceit. Yet each poor cross, occupied, robbed the
latecomers of all but the poor part of copying: and the meanest of things
were those done by example. The virtue of sacrifice lay within the
victim's soul. Honest redemption must have been free and child-
minded. When the expiator was conscious of the under-motives and the
after-glory of his act, both were wasted on him. So the introspective
altruist appropriated a share worthless, indeed harmful, to himself; for
had he remained passive, his cross might have been granted to an
innocent. To rescue simple ones from such evil by paying for them his
complicated self would be avaricious in the modern man. He, thought-
riddled, could not share their belief in others' discharge through his
agony, and they, looking on him without understanding, might feel the
shame was the manly disciple's lot: or might fail to feel it, and incur the
double punishment of ignorance. Or was this shame, too, a self-
abnegation, to be admitted and admired for its own sake? How was it
right to let men die because they did not understand? Blindness and folly
aping the way of right were punished more heavily than purposed evil, at
least in the present consciousness and remorse of man alive. Complex
men who knew how self-sacrifice uplifted the redeemer and cast down
the bought, and who held back in his knowledge might so let a foolish
brother take the place of false nobility and its later awakened due of
heavier sentence. There seemed no straight walking for us leaders in this
crooked lane of conduct, ring within ring of unknown, shamefaced
motives cancelling or double-charging their precedents.

"There is nothing loftier than a cross, from which to contemplate
the world."
Lawrence had the opportunity of many crosses, ranging upwards in
complexity from the curiously beautiful self-immolation of Tallal, after
witnessing the atrocities at Tafas. But he chose instead his long
submersion in the Air Force – "mind-suicide, by some slow task to
choke at length this furnace in my brain". It is not inappropriate to
Lawrence's most exciting spirit of self-abnegation that when he came to
die it was not on any cross at all, but on a motor-cycle.

The Spectator,
2nd August, 1935.

The Lawrence Letters

The Lawrence legend is only beginning. It is difficult to see yet how far it will reach. But I think it will expand in a way which to-day it is almost impossible to believe. I am rating it rather low if I say that I think he will be the best-remembered man of this century – of *any* nation.

To be remembered, when the civilisation in which you lived has vanished; to be the Flesh made Word: a man must be both extra-ordinary and ordinary: a summing (not an average, I *mean* a summing) of a wide and everlasting area of humanity.

It is difficult for me to say what I have to say lucidly, because it is rather out of the range of what a reviewer usually has to say; and the tongue stammers it. But you will see what I mean in contrasting an average to a summing, and calling Lawrence a *summing,* first, of the men who fought in the war, if I say that the Unknown Soldier is meant to be the *average* of the men who fought in the war.

Lawrence was a civilian suddenly flung into it, like so many. But his achievement, in the war-sphere, was as successful as a day-dream (what simple young soldier did not dream of just such a stepping-out-of-the-ranks, just such a decisive campaign won on his own in the very teeth of the professionals and the generals?). 1914: a young archaeologist. 1918: a Colonel, C.B., D.S.O., and (or so the papers said) Prince of Mecca, creator of one army and captor of another – without the loss of one English life. One of the ablest generals (a competent critic has since told us) of all time. About to be the father of three kingdoms. And then, this bright star of war was yet hollowed by a disillusion; not as great, no, far greater than that of any war poet. No soldier's hands were ever cleaner than his: no soldier ever won a campaign with fewer casualties among the enemy: but that hatred of the fruits of what he was doing which affected nearly every conscious fighting man was in him proportionate to his achievement. A lesser disillusion would have driven him to death in some desperate action. But his was too great a disillusion for that. That means, a very great disillusion.

If Lawrence's career had ended there, or taken a normal course from there, he would perhaps have been the summing of a generation. But that is not enough to be remembered alive, when the generation has passed. There have been many men, in the world's history, who have risen brilliantly on an emergency – there is nothing rare in that. But what Lawrence did next *is* rare. Other men, who have risen as high as he did, have either struggled higher or missed their hold and fallen. Lawrence neither struggled higher nor fell. He dived. He beat his way back into obscurity against greater opposition, both without and within, than he had faced when he beat his way to fame. To a level of obscurity lower than he had risen from. He used his brains to create a record of what he had done and been, itself without parallel among the autobiographies of action; and having completed that task, deliberately set out to kill his brain and his excelling. Not by a quick pistol-shot or by such physical means as drugs, but by the power of his will. You will see by the dull egotistic mediocrity of his last letters that he succeeded.

A man who excelled superlatively, and so hated his excelling that he strangled the power in him to excel. Did it so successfully, that, in the end, he even seemed to begin to want it again.

It is difficult to find a parallel in all history to that – on the same scale. It is all very well for you and me to say that we have renounced the kingdoms of this world, that we have no wish to be in any dictator's shoes. But have we ever had the chance? Not only the opportunity, I mean to say, but the capacity? Has the Devil ever taken us up into a high place, and shown us the kingdoms? He had, to Lawrence.

It is that dive, in my belief, which singles out Lawrence, and will make his legend timeless. For it is a summing of something timeless. Every successful man has hated success, and hates it, and always will hate it. But no other successful man of modern times has ever escaped back from it: at least, not without help from others, not without throwing upon his enemies the burden of his defeat.

There are those who say that Lawrence's death in a casual accident was inappropriate. I think you will not say that if you read again the hundredth chapter of *The Seven Pillars of Wisdom*. For there you will see the peculiar complexity of Lawrence's abnegation. The Devil had taken him into a high place, and offered him the kingdoms of the world and he had refused. Yes; but that, I seem to remember, has happened before . . . Then the Devil took him into a higher place – a cross – and offered him that: and he refused that too.

For the man who has renounced a cross, knowing why he did it, is a skidding motor cycle an inappropriate end?

You may think that by over-simplification I am exaggerating to an hysterical degree. Of course I am! I am doing it willingly, because I am trying to foresee the shape which the Lawrence legend will take: and why it will take it. I agree, however, that no simplified theory of Lawrence can in fact fail to be misleading, because there were so many men in that one carcase.

I knew him at his middle period, in 1920-21: when he was living partly at All Souls, and partly in London, and the suicide inwards had been determined upon but not begun. At that time you met plenty of people who were ready to tell you (all differently) what Lawrence was really like. They had seen through this layer or that, and underneath the "real" Lawrence was so-and-so. Well, you can do that with some men: peel off the skin, like the skin of an apple, and see the flesh of the fruit. But Lawrence was built more like an onion – where for every skin you peel off there is another underneath, for-ever-and-ever-Amen. There was no getting – then – at any "true" Lawrence.

But at that time at any rate (I cannot speak for any other period), his company had that peculiar quality of greatness, the quality once summed up so naively but so revealingly in the words "It is good for us to be here!" I have a memory which retains almost nothing of the life which flows by me. I can hardly remember five or six other incidents out of nearly four years at Oxford. But I can remember quite clearly every time that I was in Lawrence's company.

Bear in mind that I was as ignorant an undergraduate as could be found: I had hardly heard of him, before I met him. But one night in the summer of '21 he talked (for some reason or other) to three or four of us continuously for several hours, telling us the whole story of his life from childhood. The story, part of which became known later in *The Seven Pillars of Wisdom,* and part of which has only appeared now in these *Letters.* In spite of my unusual powers of forgetting, I think everything that he said then has remained in my memory. I recognised each incident, as it was published later. There is only one exception, one incident that I have not yet seen in print. He told us that in his Carchemish days, before the war, he was searching Aleppo for ancient objects, and stumbled one day into the house of a curio-dealer rather hurriedly – to find himself in the middle of a Secret Society meeting of Syrian Arabs (the Fetah, I suppose). At first they were very frightened of him; but he got their confidence, and so learned something of the secret Arab organisations in the Turkish Empire before ever the storm broke. That story may have appeared in print before: I do not know. I have not seen it.

At the time of Lawrence's enlistment Robert Graves wrote 'The Clipped Stater.' The fable of this poem was that Alexander, deified by his troops, had not died; but had himself translated to China by Djinns, and served there as a common soldier on the frontier. When, after many years, the arrears of pay came up, Alexander was paid in one of his own coin – a Stater, much clipped, which had somehow found its way across Central Asia.

Graves was right. It was impossible for Lawrence to escape wholly from his own past. His friends in the ranks mostly seem to have known who he was – or rather, who he had been. But it does not seem to have discommoded their relationship: or been more than a subject for mild barrack-room teasing. It was the world outside which was discommoded: the Authorities, Parliament, the world at large. For several years he was turned out of the Air Force, as if his presence might burn a hole in it. Later, when living the life of the most humdrum aircraftsman in India, he was turned out of India as if he might explode it. To such an extent had his dive, even in his lifetime, begun to propel the legend!

One cannot help wondering what might have happened if Lawrence, having reached his temporal height, had – like most men – tried to rise higher. He might have succeeded, of course, or he might not. He would have made some mistakes; for though he had genius he was not a god. (In Near-Eastern affairs, though he correctly predicted the resurrection of Turkey, he much underrated Ibn Saud – as Ibn Saud later underrated him: and he much overrated, like so many of us, the part which Anglo-French imperial rivalry would play in post-war world affairs.) But of one thing you can be certain: whatever further height Lawrence might have risen to (speaking in terms of Downing Street, or the next war) it is unimaginable that he would not now have been thought a littler man than he is thought to-day.

It may seem odd that in reviewing these *Letters* I have hardly referred to them; and quoted none of them. They are good letters: but not much more. They are not important as separate pieces of writing. Their importance is cumulative, for the light they throw on the extraordinary and complex character of the man who wrote them. In that sense, they are one of the most important collections ever to be published. For Lawrence, as he himself knew, was not an artist. What is best in an artist's mind is externalised in works of art: you can see it, there, outside – it is mere idle curiosity to peer within. But not with Lawrence. If you would see the beautiful complexity of that intensely active mind you must look *into* it: and these letters, with *The Seven Pillars of Wisdom,* are the chief means of doing so.

New Statesman & Nation, *10th December 1938.*

Robert Louis Stevenson:
a Centenary Tribute

Let 'A' be a famous novelist: which is his masterpiece? Sometimes my fingers reach of themselves for one book on the shelf. Sometimes the answer is a single character, who has grown out of his story like a child out of his breeks – Dickens I think of, surely, in terms of characters rather than books. Sometimes the answer is not found between any pair of covers. It is in the mind only, not anywhere precisely in print. It has been said of Kipling that *his* greatest work of fiction was the British Raj itself.

Now, Stevenson: a candidate for one of these high places. Ah, I start thumbing along the shelf for the immortal *Treasure Island,* do I? But it isn't there, I've put it in the children's room; and *Kidnapped* and *Catriona* too. *The Master of Ballantrae,* then? H'm: a fine beginning, but – oh, that cardboard finale in the Canadian woods! Stevenson himself feared it would "shame, perhaps degrade, the beginning". Then *Weir of Hermiston,* his last book: a grand, unfinished, unpolished torso, illumined, as Henry James puts it, "with the particular grace and sanctity of mutilation"; but it is, after all, fragmentary. I read these books – all of them – with pure, clean pleasure. But I lay them down with a feeling, somehow, that, taken one by one, they lack weight, as if clearness and light were their all. Is there, then, some wider unconscious emanation, as with Kipling? What we really experience through reading them, what we remember, isn't it Stevenson himself? Isn't this perhaps the answer, then, that the masterpiece of Stevenson's creation was 'R.L.S.'?

But that is a very odd answer. I cannot think of another case where a novelist's own personal image is more vivid in the general mind of his readers than any given one of his made characters, or any given one of his stories. Would you say the image of Dickens was a tenth as clear to you as Mr. Micawber's? We don't know the life of Defoe as we know the story of Robinson Crusoe. At this point the path grows tricky and we may trip. Stevenson is a recognised candidate for one of the high places, and in those upper levels criticism cannot go by rule; so I must beware!

Can it be right to rate an author by his own personality, rather than by his 'Mrs. X', or that famous death-scene on page thingummy? If that were so, need an author bother to write at all, can't he trust to his publicity agent and the gossip-writers? But that misses the point. It was not the publicity men and the gossips who created this 'R.L.S.' phantasm: Stevenson created R.L.S. Stevenson wrote him. There was too, of course, oceans of gossip column stuff about R.L.S. Bound to be. The Edinburgh bairn first, "not bonny, but pale, penetrating and interesting": and then the velvet jacket, the lank hair, the burning eyes in the pale indoor face, the incessant movement of the tall but feather-weight invalid's frame; the talk, talk, incessant, excited, spell-binding talk. Much was made, by others, of the smiling courage and energy of a man who seldom felt as well as we feel when we think we feel very ill: the longing for simple romantic adventure of one accustomed to face death with his back to – a pillow: "the ironic, desperate gallantry, burning away with a finer and finer fire, more touching to us from his own resolute consumption of the smoke".

Then came that spectacular last metamorphosis of the wheelchair Bohemian: "the pallid brute", he called himself, "that lived in Skerry-vore like a weevil in a biscuit". At the ebb of his strength but the top of his fame, adored by almost every literate man, woman and boy, he departed finally with wife and stepson in a schooner for the far South Seas. He went, because in any climate less balmy he knew he would die more quickly. But, truly, it was more an exodus from Europe and America than an exile (as his friends thought it). He had never loved, nor even reconciled himself to, "the prim, obliterated, polite face of life". In the Pacific, with every breath of warm air he felt better and stronger; and in the Islands, among warring Samoan tribes and poten-tates, he became at last the likeness of one of his dreamed Highland chieftains. An active chieftain; tireless and brave and paternal – but still 'Tusitala', the chiseller of legend; still writing, publishing, writing; roughing in the outline of *Weir of Hermiston,* which he knew was very good: till the bloodvessel broke in the teeming brain and with the two wondering words "What's that?" he dropped dead.

What food for biographies and memoirs, collections of letters, and reminiscences and Stevensoniana of all kinds! Yes, but I can't despise it for mere wrappings. It is part, even if only the outer part, of that towering R.L.S. image we are talking about. And I won't pause too long at what some observers professed to find next underneath; under the beloved charmer, the man who did not love his friends; under the apparent vitality, the restlessness of fever; behind the dancing smile, the private look of unplumbed despondency. Not pause too long, for that is not quite our business. I am not a biographer, tunnelling into the man, Stevenson; our concern is the phantasm, R.L.S.: not the man, but the work of art – how came it to being?

At this point I must call on another to help, as Dante took Virgil for his guide. One of the most intimate of Stevenson's friends was that very great novelist Henry James. It would be hard to find writers superficially more unlike, but James loved Stevenson the man, and truly admired the writer, and the volume in which Janet Adam Smith has collected the correspondence of these two is of very particular interest, if you care about seeing literature from the inside: ''I have been reading over *Catriona* and *Weir*'', he wrote, five years after Stevenson's death: ''I've been reading them with the purest pleasure with which we can follow a man of genius''.

On this problem of the R.L.S. image, and its peculiar part as the flower, willy-nilly, of Stevenson's creative genius, Henry James hits the nail on the head with his usual beautiful precision: ''It was as if he wrote himself altogether'', says James; ''rose straight to the surface of his prose, so that these things gave out his look and his voice, showed his life and manners, his affairs and his very secrets''. As James pointed out, it is not that Stevenson's novels were subjective, they never were: they were never about himself nor even about people at all like himself, nor did he, as narrator, step between the reader and the action: and yet, as James expounds, the effect of the stories was so commonly evocative of the writer that Stevenson's published correspondence, when it came, ''only seemed to administer delightfully a further push to a door already half open, and through which we enter with an extraordinary absence of the sense of intrusion . . . We feel indeed we are living with him: but what is that but what we were doing before? . . . We had lived with him in *Treasure Island,* in *Kidnapped* and *Catriona*''. Surely this is a far cry from the constructions of the publicity agent! This 'R.L.S.' image that Stevenson evokes in the minds of his readers: he does it by writing. Tolstoy defines art as the means by which the artist infects other people with feelings he has himself experienced. Isn't that just what Stevenson did?

But what was the stature of this R.L.S. image? What else was there besides the wrappings? Why was James, the connoisseur of personality, so deeply bound up in Stevenson? ''Stevenson never covered his tracks'', wrote James, ''and the tracks proved perhaps to be what most touches us: we follow them with the same charmed sense with which he made us follow one of his hunted heroes in the heather''. Following them, what do we find? James summed up, as it seemed to him, what he found. "Stevenson's wisdom on matters of life was really winged and inspired, a soundness . . . that it is a luxury to touch".

Now we must shift our ground a bit, from Stevenson the work of art to Stevenson the artist: for there was, too, this second link binding him to James. Stevenson, like James, was humbly and absolutely serious about the art of literature, though he once admitted himself, compared with James, when it came to performance, "a lout and a slouch". This seriousness was almost unshared by any of their prose contemporaries – I am not forgetting Hardy, Barrie, Kipling. Two against the world. Stevenson "the supremely silver of speech", wrote James in '99," . . . may well remind a vulgarised generation of what, even under its nose, English prose can be". "If it had not been for *Catriona*", he had written in '93, "we couldn't this year have held up our heads. It had been long before that since any decent sentence was turned in English".

Stevenson's words are glass. You can see the action through them almost as if there were no words between. But perhaps too much has always been said about Stevenson's prose – as if his art were only skin deep. That would be unjust. It is not the windowpane that matters so much, but what you see through it. Don't imagine that this window opens on any common view: every feature of it is conscious construction: "No art can successfully compete with life", wrote Stevenson in an essay which reveals his strength and his deficiency. "The whole secret is that no art does compete with life. Man's one method, whether he reasons or creates, is to half-shut his eyes against the dazzle and confusion of reality . . . Life is monstrous, infinite, illogical, abrupt and poignant: work of art, in comparison, is neat, finite, self-contained, flowing and emasculate . . . A proposition of geometry does not compete with life, and a proposition of geometry is a fair and luminous parallel for a work of art".

Robert Louis Stevenson was born a hundred years ago. In this centenary year books are appearing in his honour; a definitive collected edition of his verse is in the press; the Scots are audibly building a new national hero; the B.B.C. is producing a veritable pageant of Stevenson is every department. Busts, plaques and the like will no doubt play their part in the celebration. Speeches. Food and drink. But, what is the true memorial we should erect to Stevenson in this hundredth year? Go through our book shelves, pick out the bad books. Burn them – if they will burn. Then set about patiently to fill the gaps.

The Listener, *16th November, 1950*

Mr. Forster's Quandary

Here are quotations from Mr. E.M. Forster's new book, *The Hill of Devi:* "*The New Palace, Dewas. October 10th, 1921.* – Tomorrow is the 'Dassera,' the great National Festivity, and we shall have to put up a coconut in the office and worship it or eat it, I am not sure which . . . I find that the motor-cars and the electric battery each want to worship one, too. Hoping to have caught the spirit of Dassera, I then offered one to the Tennis Court, and another to the Guest House, but, no, wrong again. The Tennis Court and the Guest House never pray to coconuts, and the Garden did its ceremony about a month ago . . . *October 13th.* We are just through Dassera. I had to act the priest twice. It was enjoyable. The first time I adored a pen, an inkpot, a wastepaper basket and a piece of foolscap, under the direction of my clerk, and administered both to them and him a sacrament of coconut. The coconut kept bouncing up from the office carpet and looking at me when I tried to crack it. Then, proceeding to the Electric House, I did similar to the switchboard, the dynamo, the batteries, and the engineers. One hasn't to say anything, still less to feel. Just wave incense and sprinkle water and dab with red powder anything you like."

"Affection all through his chequered life was the only force to which Bapu Sahib responded. It did not always work, but without it nothing worked": again: "Quite often I did not understand him – he was too incalculable – but it was possible with him to reach a platform where calculations were unnecessary": and again: "His religion was the deepest thing in him," and again: "The things of this life mean so little to him – mean something so different, anyway – I never feel certain what he likes, or even whether he likes me; consideration for others so often simulates affection in him. I only know that he is one of the sweetest and saintliest men I have ever known, and that his goodness is not mawkish, but goes with deep insight into character and knowledge of the world. It is very difficult to describe him because he does belong to another civilisaton in a way that other Indians I have met do not."

What quality, what class of book then is this that Mr. Forster has given us at long last? A major work, or a delicate trifle? When an author so eminent as Mr. Forster has published so little for so long both he and his public are put in a quandary. That next book, when at last it comes – if it has any pretensions to being a major work at all, surely it will have to be something stupendous! It has to do even more than just to emulate past works already grown to exemplary status, it has as well (he and we may feel) to outweigh the accusing decades of virtual silence piled up and still piling up in the scales against him. Consequently we shall open it with jealous suspicion. The more indefatigable kind of author, the book-a-year man, is allowed his occasional lapses, to publish something inferior now and then, even a blatant pot-boiler masquerading: we permit him to be a little below par in 1953 in the hope that he will be his old self again quite early in 1954. But we can't extend any licence of this sort to the Forsters. That at least is one side of the quandary – Mr. Forster's quandary and ours. Here is a great reputation to enhance, a long period of silence to justify by its fruits. To put it as brutally as possible: if Mr. Forster cannot after all this time give us an even better book than the ones which long ago made him famous, surely he is ill-advised now to break his Trappist vows at all? Better, that in due course he should go down still dumb into the tomb?

But fortunately the quandary has quite another and a gentler aspect, another way out (as in India, where every hole you get yourself into is said to have two ends). When an author so eminent as Mr. Forster has written so little for so long, ought we not rather to be grateful for any-thing – anything at all from his golden pen? A volume of his school essays, his lecture notes, even his laundry lists? In short, for *anything* graceful, provided it makes no masquerade of being a work of the imagination, the awaited masterpiece . . . yes, that is the essential point, it must be something patently unassuming, with no pretence of being a major work.

A bundle of old travel-letters (containing interesting source-material for *A Passage to India*), for example, worked up with a few pages of commentary into a biographical sketch of an unimportant Indian prin-celing . . . what could be more unassuming, and what, in the quandary, more suitable?

We con the blurb, then, on the wrapper of the new book, and the slightly apologetic preface: we glance at the faintly "period" frontis-piece photograph of H.H. Sir Tukoji Rao III, K.C.I.E., and then – confident that we have guessed right about Mr. Forster and his famous quandary and the way out of it he has chosen – we begin to read in a totally disarmed frame of mind: with a sigh, perhaps, because we know we must not expect too much, but prepared to enjoy anything enjoyable however slight. This notion that in *The Hill of Devi* we shall be faced with deliberate triviality, will, indeed, be enhanced by some of the first

letters we read, those written during the brief 1912 visit to Dewas State:
they are readable, they are intelligent, but for the most part quite
undistinguished, and it is only in a passage of commentary that we get
our first clear glimpse of the young Maharajah himself: "His clever,
merry little face peeped out of an enormous turban: he was charming,
he was lovable, it was impossible to resist him or India."

But after a brief interlude of descriptive narrative, designed to fill the
gap between this fleeting early visit and the six months in 1921 when the
author returned to Dewas as the Maharajah's temporary private
secretary, come the 1921 letters themselves and the narrative passages
which link them. This was the period when the two men became really
intimate, and this is the backbone of the book. The letters are varied in
mood and they are vivid: the serious ones are as vividly serious as the
first batch of letters quoted at the head of this review are vividly farcical
and somewhere in the course of reading them the entranced reader
finds growing in him an uneasy feeling – has he been hoodwinked? Is
this after all literature, masquerading as something trivial?

For all the book's brevity and unassuming airs, is it the awaited
major work? It would need a critic a good deal more cocksure than the
present reviewer, and a longer period of cogitation than any reviewer
can hope for, to give an unequivocal answer to that question –
especially with so much double-bluffing in the air. For the present a few
pointers must suffice, and the reader must decide at his leisure.

It was suggested in these columns a little while ago that a proper
description of literature is to call it the self-consciousness of society.
From that point of view at any rate this book is certainly literature; for it
brings into our consciousness a way of living and feeling and thinking
and worshipping that were not there already. The Maharajah, "certainly a genius, possibly a saint, and he had to be a king": the canvas is
small, but as a character he is more vivid and more valuable than any
character in *A Passage to India,* for example: he is a person, whereas those
(no doubt deliberately) were types. An exceptional person, and the
catastrophe of his bankruptcy, his flight to Pondicherry and his death
have an imaginative as well as a historical truth which exceeds the more
contrived catastrophe of the novel.

Again, *ars est celare artem* – how is the effect produced? It is no belittle-
ment of *A Passage to India* to say that it is always possible to see "how it is
done" (which is a far cry, of course, from pretending one could do it
oneself): but the literary machinery of *The Hill of Devi* is subtler: after
reading it twice, it is still not easy to see "how it is done". There is either

consummate conjuring here, or else true magic.

One could continue quoting interminably, and yet the *effect* of the book would somehow continue to slip between one's fingers. For this effect is an effect of the whole, and not to be found in any of the parts, nor can the eye see quite *how* the parts combine to create it. Thus we are brought back to the earlier question: has an unwary reviewer allowed himself to succumb to a particularly skilful double bluff – or is this in fact a piece of *literature,* a major work of its author, something that perhaps will live in the minds of readers of a generation which shall label *A Passage to India* as no more than a skilful political tract?

The Spectator,
16th October, 1953

Virginia Woolf

Cyril Connolly was himself one of those critics who began in the Thirties to question the established reputations of Virginia Woolf and Bloomsbury's "mandarins" generally: writing in 1938, moreover, he could not then have been under the spell of the first impact of the book, for it had been published seven years earlier: yet even he described Virginia Woolf's *The Waves* as "a masterpiece": called it this ". . . group of five or six huge panels which celebrate the dignity of human life and the passage of time . . . one of the books which come nearest to stating the mystery of life, and so, in a sense, nearest to solving it."

Re-reading *The Waves* in 1953, in a different world altogether and in a period when Virginia Woolf's reputation is understandably in more general eclipse, the present writer still feels no desire to quarrel with Connolly: the book is indeed a celebration (in the sacramental sense); and a profound statement, in terms at the same time elegiac and lyrical – the work of a woman of genius. It is a masterpiece in the strict sense (the piece of work which admitted a mediaeval journeyman among the "masters").

Virginia Woolf, then, was the last great English novelist of her age . . . *if* she was a novelist at all. For convenience we call *The Waves* a novel: but is it one? About most of her other work (except perhaps *Orlando*) the difficulty is not so formidable. To a greater or lesser extent the elegiac and lyrical tones are always present, but in each of these books a story develops out of personality and the changes in personality which time wreaks; and this is typically "The Novel," even though the tones and the form of presentation may be unusual. Some of these books, moreover, are novels of a superior order. But *The Waves* – her "masterpiece" – this flower of the English language is unlike any other flower of the English language. Does it belong then to some nameless genre which it began and ended? Can we even be certain whether to call it prose or poetry?

In this volume of extracts from his wife's diaries Mr. Woolf has included a number of appraisements and impressions of her contemporaries (the eyes, however, in that remarkable, very beautiful face saw so clearly and her satiric wit was so devastating that those of us who met her must wait till we are dead, it seems, before we can safely be told what she thought of us); but for the most part he has chosen passages for their bearing on these very questions, the nature of her creative impulse and her work. Now that we can see her mind from within, then, as well as from outside, are we any nearer to an answer whether she was essentially poet or novelist? – The fact is that in this book we find much light on the question but no answer: we find only what we ought to have known, that Nature even in compounding genius shows no signs of appreciating these classifications we so love!

We learn, for example, that her method of composition was essentially poetic. Trelawny once found Shelley scribbling, and Shelley told him: "When my head gets heated with thought it boils, and throws off words and images faster than I can skim them off." Most of her work seems to have been written in a similar state of heated inspiration. Her "mind agape and red-hot from writing" – in various forms this phrase recurs frequently. This state of mind did not necessarily produce in her a Shelleyan facility: "I can't scribble fast enough to bring it all to the surface," that mood was rare with her: more often (and particularly when writing *The Waves*) it induced sweat and effort "because of the concentration": yet always "writing is the profound pleasure, being read the superficial": there was always this uncurling of the hedgehog-mind, so that its vulnerable surfaces were temporarily exposed, this heated ecstasy, in composition. Indeed, she seems to have had to restrict her hours of composition or the heated brain raced like an engine with a slipping clutch. Revision, on the other hand, was horrible to her, and yet (this again is characteristic of the poet) she did not shirk it. She had a profound consciousness of living form, of balancing part against part, of flow and pause, and spared no effort, however hateful, to hammer the metal before it cooled into the desired shape.

Again, Gautier has defined the poet as "one for whom the visible world exists": or, as an old Welsh anthracite-miner once put it: "The poet sees, and he sees, and he sees – till he's blind with seeing." Surely there have been few English writers in whom the sense of sight has been so acute, so hyper-sensitive. It is wrong to accuse her of "overloading her pages with imagery": rather (as we learn from the diaries) it is the intense reality to her of the visible world which must constantly compel the dull-eyed reader also to see, to see all the time – to see "till he's blind with seeing". In her diary she wrote: "The look of things has a great power over me . . . But what a little I can get down into my pen of what is so vivid to my eyes, and not only to my eyes: also to some nervous fibre, or fan-like membrane, in my species." The imputation of "unreality" in her writing, then, means only this, that most of us really believe in abstractions – for us the visible world does *not* exist, and we recoil instinctively from a conviction that it does.

People – as well as clouds and trees and china plates – were part of the visible world to her. What she jotted down *first* after a meeting with Geroge Moore was: "He has a pink foolish face; blue eyes like hard marbles; a crest of snow-white hair; little unmuscular hands; sloping shoulders; a high stomach; neat, purplish, well-brushed clothes . . ." and so on. But – and this is odd – in comparison with this hyper-sensitive eye her ear was apathetic. The world of her books is an almost soundless world. In the diaries we see the rooks, beating up against the wind, their wings "slicing as if the air were full of ripples and ridges and roughnesses" – but they never caw. We *see* George Moore – Lady Cunard – Lord Donegall: we are told what they say – but we never *hear* them say it. In the novels her people speak but they have no voices (so we are never quite sure whether they are speaking or thinking). This same comparative dullness of the ear apppears in the texture of her style: it is very rhythmical – that is to say, the rhythms are rather thumped, they tend to be monotonous or where the monotony is broken the breaking is simple, obvious. (This, then, would seem after all to preclude us from calling her a poet; in a poet it would be intolerable). Another important point: most of her work seems to evince no desire for compression, for extreme distillation. Again this is not necessarily even a weakness in a prose-writer, but in a poet it would be annihilating.

Form without compression may be beautiful, but it is the beauty of clouds not of poetry.

Is she a novelist, then? Arnold Bennett complained that she "could not create characters which survive." To the extent that this is true it is because (as has been hinted earlier) she was more concerned with personality than she was with character. The distinction is clear: *I* am a person, *you* are all characters: Mr. Jones's friends are aware of his character, only Mr. Jones himself can be aware of his personality. Primarily the people in her novels are seen as persons, through their own eyes: only secondarily from outside, by each other, as characters. Every great novelist, of course, is interested in personality as well as in character – the difference in her work is one of emphasis rather than of kind. But it is an important difference. Taken with what has been said already it means that whereas most novels consist of *characters* set in a world where *abstract ideas* primarily are real, hers consist of *persons* set in a *visible world* which, primarily, is real. Yet she proved that personality can engender a story just as character can: so the difference is not necessarily a disqualification of a novelist. But is something so unusual as very nearly to be one.

In most novelists' diaries one finds notes of people met, seen as possible characters; incidents related, as the possible germ of stories. But not here – where the only professional notes of the kind are visual. Her stories, then, were drawn like a spider's thread out of her own stomach. For character can be observed, but personality cannot except in oneself: every novel of personality is in an entire sense autobiographical, every person in it a facet of the author. Thus she was Rhoda – but also Susan and Jenny, Louis, Bernard and Neville . . . she was Mrs. Dalloway and she was Septimus Smith: twins of her mind's womb: only Dr. Holmes – that mere character – running up the stairs with the unforgivable word on his lips, was of alien (and prophetic) birth.

It is understandable – quite apart from the normal fluctuations of fashion – that Virginia Woolf's reputation is today rather lower than intrinsically it deserves. For one thing (as Forster has pointed out) as well as being a woman of genius she was an English lady, thus her novels are mostly about ladies and gentlemen and today taboo is strident that we should forget that ladies and gentlemen in the English sense ever existed – or remember them only as grotesques, not persons. Indeed, *Between the Acts* – one of her finest works – is the last elegy on that world, written as it fell in fragments: written in the

Kentish countryside while the Battle of Britain was being fought over her head. But more fundamentally, we live today in a world where reality is deemed more and more to be the prerogative of abstractions: the visible today is merging into the dun of the gloaming, we are losing the delight of the eye (as we have long lost the delight of the nose). It is an age too when personality (as the word is used here) is publicly at a discount, for we are striving towards group-consciousness at the expense of self-consciousness, as if that were something higher rather than the primitive thing shared with the animals from which self-consciousness had only at any time very partially emerged.

"What is to become of all these diaries, I asked myself yesterday. If I died, what would Leo make of them? He would be disinclined to burn them; he could not publish them. Well, he should make up a book from them, I think, and burn the body. I think there is a little book in them . . ." – There is indeed! A book that will be read with fascination by anyone who respects her work or who, more generally, is interested from whatever angle in the nature of literary creation. Moreover even those who are totally out of sympathy with writing and living of her kind may find a dose of it a useful corrective to the Genius of the Age. It is sensible of dogs to eat an occasional blade of grass.

Review of *A Writer's Diary*
The Spectator,
20th November, 1953

Joyce Cary

There is a monograph on Joyce Cary in the British Council's series on *Writers and their Work*. In it, Walter Allen calls Cary the "novelist and celebrant" of the creative imagination (using the term, of course, as of something not confined to artists but common to humanity). "Cary's characters," he says, "are impelled by fantasies personal in the deepest sense, unique to each one of them, which must be translated into action. Life about them is as it were so much raw material that must be shaped according to their fantasies, which are never seen as fantasies because they are so fundamental to the characters who are moved by them. And the shaping fantasy, creative imagination, is something belonging to man by virtue of his being man.''

Again, Cary himself has spoken of ''this world which is condemned to be free . . . and condemned to live by its imagination.''

The philosophical doctrines of writers need to be measured on special scales in relation to their work, and the reader will be quick to see that here is a doctrine which could be the breath of life to a novelist, at any rate to a novelist with the powers of invention and the deeply penetrating sympathy of Cary. This is indeed a ''faith'' by which such a novelist can be ''justified''. In a less inventive writer it could lead merely to the aridities of the Commedia dell'Arte (or of D.H. Lawrence at his worst): the typical character, whose fantasy is a precise formula – once the formula is mastered, his reactions can always be forecast. But Cary's characters (we must not forget) are ''condemned to be *free*'' as well as condemned to mould life to their fantasies. ''The weakest child'', says Cary, ''has power and will. It can be commanded, but it need not obey.'' Thus all Cary's characters, however compelling their fantasy, preserve their freedom of will. The reader can never hope to forecast of a Cary character however clear-cut what he will do or feel next. In short, what comes ''next'' is never a recapitulation, always a further revelation. Hence Cary derives that power of pleasurable suspense which carries the reader from the first page of some long and intricate novel of his unflaggingly to the last, and the fact that his characters remain, to the end, lifelike.

But although because of this emphasis on freedom of will his characters remain lifelike, it is a natural result of his emphasis on the creative imagination that they should all be a little larger than life-size. Granted that in life the creative imagination is the power in us, in life it is nevertheless so dolefully overlaid with a contrary element of passivity and behaviourism that it is a spark or ember, usually, rather than a fire. It follows too from the Cary approach that he is able to take the most reprehensible creatures, Tabitha Basketts and Gully Jimpsons and Ninas, and to let them perform actions whose enormity is – well, enormous, without shocking. We follow these people from one outrageous action to the next with a sense of deepening understanding, of deepening sympathy, of . . . *love*. Not love in the sense of favouritism, but of Charity – and not Charity in the sense of ''making allowances'', but in the noblest, the full Pauline sense of a total empathy. There is no question of "making allowances", entire and as they are they are the objects of Cary's Charity, and so of ours. One could almost say that his purpose is "To justify the ways of man to God." At least, this is the case so long as their fantasy is single-minded – the eye of the imagination *single*. Gully Jimpson of *The Horse's Mouth* is cracked, he is criminal, he is a person impossible to befriend, there is no sentimental or romantic word to be said for him, there is no evidence but his own that he is a painter of genius – yet his figure is illuminated by a nimbus of that blessedness we associate with sainthood because his life, like the saint's, is one unceasing struggle conducted with all his might along one straight path towards one blinding illuminant (hence the nimbus: the grimy figure is always seen as it were against the centre of that light).

Yes, certainly it is that singleness of the eye of the imagination which is the secret. For in Cary's last book, *A Prisoner of Grace,* we were shown in equal detail Chester Nimmo, a sincere evangelical Christian and a reforming radical statesman who rose to power from poverty and obscurity – and we hate him. There is no change in Cary's method and Cary's impartiality. Nimmo is seen (through the eyes of his wife Nina) with the same penetrating sympathy from our first meeting with the class-conscious young estate-clerk and lay-preacher with aspirations to the County Council, the intuitive young husband handling his monstrous honeymoon with consummate skill; and when we are about to close the book on Lord Nimmo the fallen cabinet minister, his incipient megalomania and its concomitant senile sexuality are still described with sympathy and understanding. Yet this time there is no nimbus: rather, the epitaph which filters naturally into the mind is that verse from *Acts* which describes the death of Herod Agrippa when, with the words of his last Oration hardly out of his mouth, "The Angel of the Lord smote him and he was eaten of worms and gave up the ghost."

The lifelong worms which corrupted the flesh of Chester Nimmo were the worms of "double-think": his creative imagination was cursed with double-vision. Thus he was not even a hypocrite: "Hypocrisy is a very rare vice," says Nina, "people do not need to be hypocrites." Chester's wrath against the rural poverty of his day "was quite sincere: his cleverness was in choosing the right thing to be angry about . . . Chester's imagination suggested to him every day hundreds of truths and it was always easy for him to find among them one which 'suited' him."

In short, we expect to find a clash, in the reforming statesman, sooner or later, between ideals and expediency: a moral conflict: but in

Nimmo a moral conflict was impossible, because he always followed his conscience – confident that his conscience would never urge him on an inexpedient course.

The character of Nimmo has been dwelt on here because he – the principal "object" in *A Prisoner of Grace* – becomes the "subject," the narrator, in Cary's new novel *Except the Lord*. This is a favourite device of Cary's and usually a successful one: the shift of viewpoint adds solidity, the two pictures however different are recognisably two aspects of one whole – a "3D" effect. The new book, then, is presumably to be regarded as the first volume of those memoirs the old man was so busy on, written after his fall from power (but surely before his divorce). It describes – at times, brilliantly – his Victorian childhood of poverty in the Devon countryside. It tells (and this is a nice paradoxical touch) how his sense of social injustice was first aroused not by the life around him but by a fair-booth performance of *Maria Marten,* and how this same performance, rather than his father's eloquent chapel-sermons, first opened his eyes to the power of the spoken word. It describes his early flirtations with various political "-isms", culminating in Marxist trade union politics, and, after he had burned his fingers in that fire, his recovery of the evangelical faith he had been brought up in. Historically it ends where the other book begins.

Historically, too, the account is credible and satisfying. These are the kind of beginnings out of which the character of Chester Nimmo could have developed. And yet it is a question of character which is likely to prove to the reader of both books a fatal stumbling-block. Not the character of the young man written about, but the implied character of the old man deemed to be doing the writing. The gap between this memoir-writing Chester Nimmo and the Chester Nimmo of *A Prisoner of Grace* is too wide: even with our "3D" spectacles on, the two images remain obstinately separate. Surely that Nimmo was too far gone in disintegration to have assumed the benignity that we feel in the present narrator, this philosophical detachment and tolerance? Again, the vividest passages in the present book all conjure up some *other* figure: the forlorn baby stretching up its hands by its mother's death-bed, that turbulent and steadfast child his sister Georgina – even that unfortunate middle-aged baby Fred Coyte. Is it credible that the cunning old-stager would ever in his own memoirs have allowed the limelight to be stolen from himself like this?

In short, this device of the shifted view-point seems to have let the author down, for once, and we are impelled to speculate on the cause.

Possibly it is to be found in Cary's methods of work. We are told that his habit is not to finish one book before beginning another, to work on several manuscripts at once. Perhaps, then, this new book derives from an earlier conception of Nimmo than that of the latter part of *A Prisoner of Grace:* perhaps much of this book was written and the character of the narrator unalterably "set" before the final developments of the other book were decided on. This is merely a surmise, of course – but the very fact any surmise seems called for . . .

In that case we should not consider this book as a counterpart, but in isolation. We should forget *A Prisoner of Grace.* We must forget too the unfortunate blurb on the wrapper of the book itself, which tells us that its subject is "the religious nature of man". This is a howling misnomer, for the religion of Chester Nimmo has the simplicity of extreme superficiality, not of depth. Well? – A *château* wine, certainly: unmistakable *Château Cary:* but not a vintage year. Good as it is, it would be unfortunate if the reader not familiar with Cary should suppose that this is the best he can do. Cary has not all the virtues, it is true: possibly his is a wine which will not keep, for example he lacks in his language "that suffused beauty" which has been described as "the true preservative of literature" (his language is no more than adequate: in the sense that a writer is one in whose hands words have a life of their own he is scarcely to be called a "writer"). But in this phylloxera-smitten age of the English novel it is heartening to find anyone of anything like Cary's distinction writing novels at all.

Review of *Except the Lord*
The Spectator,
18th December, 1953

George Borrow: Victorian Rebel

The Victorian Age is usually looked on as an age of conformity. Perhaps it was: otherwise it could hardly have bred so many and such great eccentrics, men who invented their own "recipes for living" instead of being content to follow Mrs. Grundy-Beeton in their ethical cooking. Of this particular class of Eminent Victorians one of the most interesting, and one of the greatest, is George Borrow.

He had an extraordinary physique. Inches over six feet tall, he had the frame and the science of a prize-fighter in an age when prize-fighters *hit*. He could ride a horse, break a horse, shoe a horse, sell a horse. As a young man he walked from Norwich to London on a mouthful of sand-wiches: in his fifties he could still walk forty or fifty miles in a day, at seventy he could still bathe in winter. He had hypnotic black eyes, an aquiline nose, hair white from boyhood and the voice of an intolerant corncrake.

He had an extraordinary brain, a memory that never forgot a foreign word once learned or a casual face once seen. He could speak and read twenty languages, from Latin and Greek to Welsh, Romany and Armenian, by the time he was twenty – thereafter one rather loses count, but it seems to have taken him a matter of weeks to learn even Manchu-Tartar, enough to edit the Gospels in that language and print them in Chinese characters. In English he composed with difficulty and very slowly: his use of the English language is sometimes singularly insensitive: but he wrote at least three books which rank today among the outstanding books of the nineteenth century.

He had an extraordinary personality. He hated "respectability-cant" and all its practitioners. His hatred of Roman Catholicism was nearly insane. He loved gypsies, peasants, thimble-riggers, prize-fighters, even murderers if he approved the motive, hedge-preachers: in fact everyone of spirit outside the respectability-pale. These were the people he chose to live with, whether as a travelling tinker in Stafford-shire or as a hard-riding evangelist in war-riven Spain. To the gypsies he became something almost more than human: a myth among the Romany tribes everywhere from Mitcham Common to Moscow. He seemed able to tame anything, from an English adder to a Spanish archbishop – murderers, mules, anything except literary ladies.

His best book is *The Bible in Spain*. It depicts the only time in his life when as a man of action he was fully stretched, and so happy: peddling Bibles among the Carlist bullets, reappearing to confront statesmen, pitted single-handed against government and church before the back-ground of an awful landscape, of a proud and ancient nation sunk into anarchy. But probably the book most read today is *Wild Wales*. It was the first book by an Englishman to take Welsh character and Welsh literature seriously as well as Welsh scenery (Borrow rated ap Gwilym above Ovid and above Chaucer). It is still one of the best books to read about Wales. It makes that Wales of a hundred years ago more vivid and more real to the modern reader than the Wales of 1954 under his nose; and in this book some of the bonnet-bees which buzz tediously elsewhere are muted.

But the book which has had most influence, even indirectly on people who have never heard of it, is *Lavengro*. For *Lavengro* and its sequel *The Romany Rye* first opened the life of the English road, the romance of gypsies and tinkers, horse-fairs and hedgerows, to the Respectable Reader. It is irony that this fashion for the 'Open Road' and the English countryside in English picaresque which the Papist-hating Borrow started should have been exploited pre-eminently by Belloc and Chesterton – Roman Catholics both.

In everything Borrow wrote he himself is the most conspicuous figure. Yet he is not a boastful writer: he wrote himself *in,* he did not particularly write himself *up;* there are plenty of contemporary witnesses that he cut at least as impressive a figure in other eyes as he did in his own. There are two chief kinds of great traveller. One is the chameleon sort which disappears against any background. Sir Richard Burton in the brothels of Scinde or the deserts of Arabia not only wore the clothes and complexion of a native, he thought like a native: his disguise was impenetrable because it went right down to the soul. Borrow is of the opposite kind. He was conspicuous everywhere: everyone was interested in him and so played up to him. Burton drew out the truth by sympathy, Borrow struck it out by contrast. In this attempt we are making to bring Borrow the enigmatic Victorian rebel to speak into the microphone of 1954 that, I think, is the chief thing which emerges: the figure of a man which fits into no known picture, a man who is *nowhere at home.*

Radio Times,
3rd December, 1954

Dylan Thomas – The Real Tragedy

When Dylan Thomas died a few months ago in his fortieth year more mourning was evoked in the general world than the death of any other ''young'' poet for a very long time had prompted. Yet he was no longer exactly young. The volume of his *Collected Poems* (1952) covers eighteen years' work, and that is a *long* creative span for a lyric poet (Keats would survive on one years' output alone). For lyric poems of this intensity are phoenix eggs that tend to scorch and cauterise even if they do not outright consume the sensitive bird which lays them.

No, what makes Dylan's ending matter so deeply is not the death of a promising young man: he was that ten times rarer thing, a promising · middle-aged man. He died in the very throes of a profound maturing, of growth from a private poet into a public one, from *clerwyr* to *pencerdd,* from the lyric and personal mode to what was virtually an epic mode. He might have become the only poet of our age of epic size. The disaster is that of this new Dylan *Under Milk Wood* should be virtually all we have.

This posthumous "play for voices" is a major work: that is unquestionable. It is of a different kind and class from any poetry he had written before, deriving as much from the spirit of his prose *Portrait of the Artist as a Young Dog* as from the general run of his verse. In the preface to his *Collected Poems* he said he had composed them "for the love of man and in praise of God". But the preface is usually the last thing in a book to be written, and in that statement I think he was looking forward rather than back, at the work he was then engaged on even more than the work he was republishing. For it is abundantly true of some, but only of some, of his lyrics; it is the clearest possible definition you could have of the attitude, the motif of *Under Milk Wood,* this "impression for voices", this "entertainment out of the darkness of the town I live in".

The town he lived in was Laugharne. It was a fortunate fate that brought Dylan to settle in Laugharne as a very young man. He fell deeply in love with it at once. He revelled like an intoxicated whirligig in the profoundly humane eccentricities of that unparalleled little township; they ran in at his five senses and out at his mouth day and night. Laugharne took the young bard to its uninhibited heart. His landlord obligingly did his laundry. Creditors secretly left offerings of green vegetables on his doorstep. Even the watching eye of the police-man was moist with appreciation the night Dylan thumped a certain tiresome head on the cobbles – so palpably was Dylan doing it "for the love of man and in praise of God". Laugharne was made for Dylan, and Dylan for Laugharne.

Like all major works, *Under Milk Wood* had a long gestation. It could grow to its final mature form only as its creator himself grew big enough. Back in the thirties, there was to be a play about Laugharne acted in Laugharne by the characters themselves – each in his own part. Then (the point at which Daniel Jones in his introduction takes up the story) came the comedy plot, the town that was to be certified insane . . . still the idea was to use some of his fellow-townsmen recognisably, for those needed no exaggeration or invention to make such a play plausible, only selection to make it sizeable.

Then, as late as 1952, came the final steps to make the play as we have it: the abandonment of the comedy plot and – even more important – the total abandonment of particular "true" portraits. For the characters of *Under Milk Wood,* vivid as they are, are not particular – they are universal, as universal as the characters in Chaucer's *Prologue:* they ought to live in Laugharne, perhaps, but in fact not one of them does. If you go to Laugharne you may say "Yes – this is Llareggyb"; what you won't be able to say is "There goes Dai Bread – there goes Polly Garter". That, I think, is the measure of the greatness of this piece of writing, which gives it a quality almost as timeless as the quality of the *Prologue* itself.

It comes as an anti-climax to say that in the short history of sound radio no other piece of comparable stature has been written for the blind art. But it was written for that medium; it has been produced and recorded, and there have been several repeat broadcasts. By radio standards it was an exceptional production. B.B.C. methods preclude the possibility of a *great* production at any time; but at least this one got the play across in outline, even if the individual flowering of words and phrases and turns of character was sometimes lost. I should like to end, then, with a plea to the B.B.C. – as an exception, for I know there are commercial reasons why they cannot make it a practice – to release *this* record on the market, so that this play for voices can be heard, as it was meant to be heard; can . . . entertain us, out of darkness.

Review of *Under Milk Wood,*
Sunday Times,
7th March, 1954

Laughter from the Doldrums

In the days of sail every ship essaying to cross the line knew the doldrums, where the winds grow fitful or fail altogether, the sails slap like cannon-fire and the very sea seems glue. It is not the good ship's fault. Even great writers have passed through a similar experience: the creative imagination is intact and aching to be put to use, but for a while the *wind* doesn't blow.

Dylan Thomas seems to have been in his doldrums when he began to write the abortive novel of which the first four draft chapters have now been published.

He showed them to a publisher at the time, and when the latter proved discouraging some at least of his friends secretly were not sorry. For this seemed perilously like writing for writing's (or even the pot's) sake. There are passages of brilliant comic invention: particularly the adventure of the tricky young nymphomaniac in the bathroom, the premises of the Paddington furniture-dealer, the bottle on the finger: but somehow, somewhere behind the belly-laughs there lurks dullness, because inherent in it all there is a battling against reality rather than a transcending of it which I find nowhere else in Dylan's writing before or since. As the work of some unknown Waughish young man, doubtless we would have hailed its promise: but not from our nonpareil, the poet of *25 poems* and *The Map of Love,* whose completely satisfactory stories had just been collected in *Portrait of the Artist as a Young Dog*! The humanist, in whom the seeds of *Under Milk Wood* were already sown! Even the never-dull midnight talker we all knew.

Part of him at least saw this. In May 1941 he wrote from my home (where he was then living and writing) to Vernon Watkins: "My prose-book's going well, but I dislike it. It's the only really dashed-off piece of work I remember doing . . . It's indecent and trivial, sometimes funny, sometimes mawkish, and always badly written which I do not mind so much."

What is the nature of this spiritual doldrums which can so bedevil a fine poet? I think it usually comes when the *Zeitgeist* pulls one way and the poet, for a time, still pulls another. This was 1941. Dylan was a native of the Thirties; but they were over, and the Thirties and the Forties of this Century were . . . centuries apart. *No* poet so sensitive to atmosphere as Dylan could have successfully written a book of this kind

– this Thirtyish kind – in these islands, against the pull of the atmosphere of the twelve months following Dunkirk. Not even in a summerhouse at Laugharne.

If not *then,* should it be published now? I think his executors have decided rightly. Parts are uproariously funny. The collector of Dylan will want his collection to be complete – and there is all too little. And we know, *now,* the poet's greatness at his best too well for any danger he will be judged down by this second-best: this "good old 3-adjectives-a-penny, belly-churning Thomas", as he called himself, "the Rimbaud of Cwmdonkin Drive".

Review of *Adventures in the Skin Trade,*
Sunday Times,
11th September, 1955

On Welsh Literature

"We have to realise" – it is a Whitehall blue-book I am quoting – "that from the very first beginnings of its history *Welsh has been one of the great literary languages of the world* . . . not to be measured by the subordinate and insignificant political position of the country where it is spoken."

More could hardly be said of Ancient Greek itself! It is one thing to be asked to recognise the independent existence of a literature, but a different kettle of fish altogether to have to include Wales among the literary "Great Powers". Can it be justified? The reader will expect a reasoned answer that he can test for himself.

Except for Sir Idris Bell's valuable contribution on the twentieth century, the 500 close-packed, learned and readable pages of Dr Parry's History were originally written in Welsh for Welshmen: we cannot, therefore, expect an *explicit* answer from Dr Parry. But a brief one, I suggest, is this.

Remember we are not here concerned with Welshmen (such as

Dylan Thomas) who have written in English. But even within the
Welsh language itself there have developed not one kind of literature
only but concurrently *two*. One of these is a general literature which is a
recognisable, reputable member of the great European family – but
only a junior one. Its affinities are by no means exclusively English:
indeed, only during its nadir in the nineteenth century did English
influences even predominate (today, Shakespeare and Eliot are
performed in Welsh translations, but so are Molière, Ibsen, Chekhov,
Anhouilh). It is remarkable, individual authors would certainly be read
and reputed if they were available, but it cannot really rival the giants,
either in bulk or majesty.

But the other is unique: for it carries certain chosen aesthetic values
beyond any point even attempted as yet by other members of the
family. It is on *this*, then, that any superlative claim (Borrow's rating of
Dafydd ap Gwilym "above Ovid and above Chaucer" is another
example) must be based. But its very uniqueness makes its "greatness"
difficult to assess – this is virtually a new art-form, a development from
the art of poetry which is virtually a "Metapoetic"; and measuring it by
the familiar standards of European poetry is very like trying to measure
pints with a yard-stick.

Wondering how so notable a development came about and at the
direction it took, there are two exceptional factors to bear in mind: the
remarkable longevity of Welsh literature, and the sensitiveness of the
Welsh ear. Welsh is easily the oldest living language in Europe with an
unbroken populous literary history. There is poetry extant from the
sixth century, and no succeeding period (including the present, thank
God) is unrepresented in the canon. But even before Caesar landed
there were British *bardoi* at work, Posidonius reports; and indeed, the
extant poetry itself bears evidence of tradition – these are no primitive
rumblings, but conscious art. Some early poems, intensely dramatic in
form and content, read almost like fragments of lost tragedies of which
only the great speeches had been preserved.

Thus, by the Middle Ages, Welsh had already a longer history than
English literature has even today! Dafydd ap Gwilym and Chaucer
were contemporaries: but already since Aneurin eight fruitful centuries
had elapsed; Chaucer was founding a new language when Dafydd and
his age were raising one long-established to new heights of beauty and
exquisiteness. Now when a literature grows as old as that, either it must
wilt and die or it *must* strike out new.

This is what happened. The difficulty of translating the earliest poems into English is primarily one of language – Old Welsh hard and compressed and whippy like steel, English more like malleable wrought iron; the underlying aesthetic of those poems feels familiarly "European". Later the language was even further tempered – for the glint and hardness of steel, the brilliance and even greater hardness of diamond; but now, even by the thirteenth century, the aesthetic itself is growing unfamiliar! Perhaps it is a fair analogy to say that we begin to feel safer with the canons of music than those of poetry. "Tongue-music" (as distinguished from tonal music) is how the Welshman himself classifies it. Moreover, like music it is a social not a private art (hence the Eisteddfod).

Remember that this was a people ancestrally gifted with an exceptionally sensitive ear. By the twelfth century they had been playing and singing harmony "from time immemorial", says the traveller Giraldus, and he was hard put to it to convey to a Europe still stuck at unison how the Welsh could sound *different* notes together and yet know them sweet. Similarly the Welshman today is at a loss to convey to outsiders the ecstatic pleasure his trained ear takes in the intricate sound-patterns of *cynghanedd*. Nowadays Europe has outstripped Wales in the development of tonal music; but in this tongue-music others have scarcely even started. For it is essentially a formal and communally recognised, not personal or voluntary art; the elaborate interlocking of echoed sounds in *cynghanedd* follows rules as rigorous as the intervals of tonal harmony. To compare the "music" of Keats with that of Dafydd ap Gwilym and his fellows is like comparing bird-song with a fugue.

Usually literatures first find recognition in translation. But how translate at all, where meaning is proportionately no more than the theme in a symphony? Even translated, there is more than a hint that the *cywyddau* of Dafydd are great poetry in the ordinary sense. But judging them in translation is like judging opera by libretto without score.

The interested reader will find Dr Parry's History invaluable, but I would advise him to study Mr Gwyn Williams's brilliant and enthusiastic *Introduction to Welsh Poetry* first. It is directly aimed at the English reader, and the field being narrower the focus is perhaps clearer. But in the long run there is no help for it – we shall all have to learn Welsh! Welsh has survived today as a spoken language, against all the odds, because it is still written. So long as its literature continues to evolve vitally, it will continue to be spoken. But if ever that ceases and it becomes a mere vernacular, a mere mother-tongue, I would not give it one more generation's purchase; it is because it is a great literary language that is survives.

Review of *A History of Welsh Literature*
by Thomas Parry, with an Appendix on the
Twentieth Century by H. Idris Bell; and
An Introduction to Welsh Poetry
by Gwyn Williams
Sunday Times,
January, 1956

Faulkner and Bennett

This was written in 1929:

> If I were asked who seems to me at the moment the most interesting novelist in America, I should not hesitate in naming one who is not only unknown in England but is practically unknown in America also – William Faulkner. He is a Southerner, from Mississippi: young, prolific, and unsuccessful . . .
>
> Faulkner . . . in his native State . . . follows the solid calling of a house-painter, producing at the same time out of the natural fecundity of his spirit novel after novel to be dropped by hesitant publishers into an ungrateful world.

This passage comes from a preface to the British edition (1930) of *Soldiers' Pay*.

By 1929, Faulkner's early novels had indeed stirred scarcely a ripple and consistently had left his publishers in the red. In New York he had brought out *The Marble Faun* in 1924, *Soldiers' Pay* (said to be the first in order of writing) in 1926, and *Mosquitoes* in 1927; but by 1929 the first two were already out of print and unobtainable because no bookseller could even be bothered to pick up second-hand copies. In that same year *Sartoris* and *The Sound of the Fury* though announced were still with the printers. The only Faulkner novel obtainable anywhere was *Mosquitoes* – and that, only if you knew where to look for it.

I recall hearing *The Marble Faun* spoken of – once – by my friend Francesco Bianco in New York in 1924; but in my muddled way half thought he was talking about Hawthorne, and had omitted to read it.

But one of the several New York publishers who took turns those days at bearing the financial burden of publishing Faulkner was Harrison Smith. Back again in America in 1929, that summer saw me cruising on the New England coast with Hal Smith. For a while his little yacht was fog-bound in Nantucket. To pass the time I regaled him with Evelyn Waugh's *Decline and Fall;* and in return he gave me Faulkner's *Mosquitoes* to read, then *Soldiers' Pay,* and then – since fortunately the fog still had not lifted – *The Sound and the Fury* in galley-proof.

A warm recommendation went home to Chatto & Windus (my own London publishers) to stake an interest in Faulkner. Of the three books read in Nantucket *Soldiers' Pay* seemed the best one to launch him with in England; but it was impossible to send them a copy since none was obtainable. All that could be sent was my own copy of *Mosquitoes* and an uncorrected set of *The Sound and the Fury* proofs.

Returning to England, I found that autumn that Chatto & Windus still had not quite made up their minds to take the plunge. This was understandable. Even successful American authors tended at that time to be found rather unappetising small-beer by British readers – and this one had not even made good in America. Moreover, this was not just a question of buying a single book but of bombarding Britain with a new and obviously prolific novelist – and a copy of the very book recommended for the opening salvo could not anywhere be found. No one in New York – not his agent, nor the book's American publisher – seemed even able to rustle up a copy of *Soldiers' Pay* to lend them to read. It was hardly surprising that no deal had yet been clinched.

But those were the days when Arnold Bennett was running his book-column each week in the *Evening Standard.* Bennett had then a greater influence on book-sales than any other critic before or since (people trusted him particularly because his critical style was so open and commonsensical: it was never his way to puff or over-praise a book, however much it had interested him). Being fresh from America, Bennett asked me one night at dinner what was new there, and scribbled the name ''Faulkner'' on his hard evening cuff.

Apparently Bennett wrote off at once to New York ordering the entire Faulkner *oeuvre.* But by this time even *Mosquitoes* had quite disappeared: the only novel now obtainable was *The Sound and the Fury,* just out. On December 19th, 1929, Bennett's column ended as follows:

I will close by giving you an example of a novel which, good or bad, was worth publishing . . . *The Sound and the Fury,* by William Faulkner. . . Having heard, from an Englishman of course, of the promise of William Faulkner, I sent to New York for all his works. But I could only get this one. The author is evidently young. He evidently has great and original talent. Influenced by James Joyce, he is exasperatingly, unimaginably difficult to read. He seems to take a malicious pleasure in mystifying the reader. The first part of his novel is supposed to be written by a deaf-mute who is also a lunatic! But William Faulkner may emerge from this youthful stage of eccentricity. If he does, he will emerge into wide appreciation. Infuriated as I am by the book, I would not have missed it.

From Bennett that was enough. Chatto & Windus made up their minds in a final split second, Charles Prentice telephoned Curtis Brown while the lunch-time *Standard* was still wet from the presses and ''bought'' Faulkner – including *Soldiers' Pay,* which he still had not seen.

On June 26th, 1930, Bennett reviewed *Soldiers' Pay* at length:

Last year I made some fuss in this column concerning the young American novelist, William Faulkner, who had been mentioned to me in conversation by Richard Hughes, author of *A High Wind in Jamaica.* No American, and even no American publisher, whom I asked about Faulkner, had ever heard of him. I sent to New York for his books, but could get only one, *The Sound and the Fury,* and that not without difficulty. Strange that Americans have frequently to be told by Englishmen of their new authors!

The first printed fuss made about Theodore Dreiser's first book was made by an Englishman. *Sister Carrie* fell flat in the United States until a review of it by myself was republished there. Then Americans said: ''Who is this man Dreiser?'' and *Sister Carrie* began to sell in America. That was thirty years ago[1]. Yet Americans say that English critics sniff at American novels.

Now Faulkner is getting a show in England. His first book, *Soldiers' Pay,* has just been published here, with a preface by Richard Hughes. His second and third will follow. *Soldiers' Pay* is labelled ''Not a war-book.'' I call it a war-book. Its chief male characters are returned soldiers, and the whole story hinges on a terribly scarred aviator, who dies of war. Also war-scenes are directly described in the book, and very well described. Unless Faulkner runs off the rails, as some young men do, but as he probably will not, *Soldiers' Pay* will be an extremely valuable collector's item in twenty years' time. Faulkner is the coming man. He has inexhaustible invention, powerful imagination, a wond'rous gift of characterisation, a finished skill in dialogue; and he writes generally like an angel. None of the arrived American stars can surpass him in style when he is at his best.

But praise of *Soldiers' Pay* must not be unreserved. It is a first book, and has the usual defects of a first book. It is clumsily constructed, being lop-sided . . . To read it demands an effort (the effort is adequately rewarded). There is no excuse for this. The great masters are not difficult to read. You know what they mean, and in their passages of dialogue you know who is saying what. In too many novels of young authors a mathematical calculation, a counting of speeches, is needed to find out who is talking. A novel ought to be easy to read; it ought to please immediately. But too many young novelists seem to be actuated by a determination not to please . . .

In this matter, Faulkner is not guiltless. To get his full value involves some heavy work for the reader. But he is the most promising American novelist known to me; more promising than, for instance, Ernest Hemingway, author of the splendid *Farewell to Arms*. He has in him the elements of real greatness, and *Soldiers' Pay* contains many quite marvellous pages . . .

In America, the effect of Bennett's article seemed to be even more electric than in England. This was *Sister Carrie* over again. Perhaps it nettled them that a British critic should discover an American author before they had discovered him themselves: at any rate (whether *propter hoc* or merely *post hoc*), Faulkner now became a best-seller in his own country; and certainly he never lacked appreciation thereafter.

Success would of course have come to Faulkner sooner or later in any case, whether or not Arnold Bennett had written about him. A hundred other chances could have triggered it. The most one can claim for the accidentals of this little anecdote is that maybe they speeded it up: perhaps by as much as a year or two.

At that time, American letters seemed ripe for the emergence of a new outstanding figure. In my preface to the British edition of *Soldiers' Pay* had been written:

The novel in America at the moment seems to have passed into a sort of interregnum. Generations change quickly there: and names only recently become really familiar in England – Lewis, Dreiser, Cabell, Wilder – seem there already to be looming with the vague bigness of the past rather than any actual, growing stature of the present. Nor has any whole generation taken their places; only a few separate writers, first among whom one immediately thinks of Hemingway . . . but even Hemingway, perhaps, has now done the work by which he is most likely to be remembered.

The times were propitious.

Faulkner never quite got over what Bennett called his "youthful eccentricity", but the reader came to accept it as typically "Faulkner". He remained rather difficult to read to the end, even in the trivial ways Bennett had pin-pointed, and also through expansiveness and over-statement and long parenthetical passages. In part this difficulty may have been deliberate. Indeed it is arguable that requiring a constant effort from the reader on a superficial level keeps that reader awake and on the *qui vive,* so that he is alert to whatever may be really difficult at profounder levels of meaning. But in part (at any rate in his earlier work) it was due to his intoxication with words, since often this was an idolatrous obeisance before words he only hazily understood and sometimes had flatly misunderstood. Such words were bound to obscure the sense of any passage in which they occurred – and they recurred with the cumulative constancy of Homeric epithets, at least in those early books of his.

But I never discussed this with Faulkner: indeed I never met him or even exchanged letters with him; and I don't think Bennett did either.

There seems to be a vein of sentimentality in every man: in every novelist, more than most. Some writers are afraid of it, just as some men are afraid of cowardice and so do desperately brave things simply to spite it: similarly these writers write desperately unsentimentally to deny and spite that vein they are only too aware of in themselves. Only a few look at it squarely, and give it a little rein deliberately, now and then, rarely and very sparingly and under strict control (like letting the dog out for a little run). I am thinking particularly of Homer, and Tolstoy. That way it does their work no harm at all. But for every writer with the gifts of a great writer there must surely come, when he becomes a "great" writer, a moment of terrible temptation to let his suppressed sentimentalism rip. Surely, he thinks, his genius will carry it off: he can allow himself an indulgence which would wreck any less writer – and he lets go.

After many years, I have just been re-reading Faulkner's *Mosquitoes* immediately after reading his book *The Reivers*. Both books show that his "wond'rous gift of characterisation" could be applied outstand-ingly to comic ends. The earlier one is brilliant satirical comedy but poignantly loving and youthful: the later one, brilliant romantic comedy of a broader, picaresque kind. I prefer the earlier book but do not under-estimate *The Reivers*. The Faulkner who wrote *The Reivers* had still those magnificent gifts: the same ''wond'rous gift of character-isation'' – an endless supply of new characters pouring down his sleeves like a cascade of aces: the same ''inexhaustible invention'' in the twists and surprises of his story (what an Ealing film this book would have made!): at his best, he still ''writes like an angel''. The scene at the mud-hole is unforgettable, and there are others nearly as good. But he allows himself depths of sentimentalism in this book about whores, and even more fundamentally about boys – the narrator is supposed to be a boy: depths of which any writer big as well as little ought to be ashamed. At times he seems to have lost all sensitivity to the difference between sentimentality and truth. The result is a partly corrupted book. It is well worth reading; but reading it is like eating a magnificent apple which has gone rotten in small patches though the firmness and flavour of most of the flesh is exquisite still.

Note

1. 1900. The book was suppressed. Wells and Walpole as well as Bennett praised *Sister Carrie,* but Dreiser did not really win wide popular acclaim till 1925 with his *An American Tragedy.* Meeting Dreiser *téte-à-téte* once in 1929 he struck a young visitor as bulky, elderly, a bit dreary, and very bewildered.

Encounter XXI, 3
September, 1963

Bibliography

This is by no means a complete bibliography. Considerations of space and relevance have led me to omit sections on individual Poems and Stories. Texts of published broadcasts appear among Articles. The sections Prefaces, Articles and Reviews are as full as possible for the present time. The Books section limits itself to English first editions, with the exception of *An Omnibus*.

Books

Gipsy-Night and Other Poems: Golden Cockerel Press, 1922.
The Sisters' Tragedy and three other plays: Heinemann, 1924.
Confessio Juvenis (collected poems): Chatto & Windus, 1926.
A Moment of Time (stories): Chatto & Windus, 1926.
A High Wind in Jamaica: Chatto & Windus, 1929.
An Omnibus: Harper and Brothers, 1931.
The Spider's Palace (children's stories): Chatto & Windus, 1931.
In Hazard: Chatto & Windus, 1938.
Don't Blame Me (children's stories): Chatto & Windus, 1940.
The Administration of War Production (with J.D. Scott): HMSO/Longmans, Green & Co., 1955.
The Fox in the Attic: Chatto & Windus, 1961.
The Wooden Shepherdess: Chatto & Windus, 1973.
The Wonder-Dog (collected children's stories): Chatto & Windus, 1977.
In the Lap of Atlas (stories): Chatto & Windus, 1979.

Editing

Poems by John Skelton, with an Introduction: Heinemann, 1924.

Prefaces

Soldiers' Pay by William Faulkner: Chatto & Windus, 1930.
The Sound and the Fury by William Faulkner: Chatto & Windus, 1931.
The Unexpected by Frank Penn-Smith: Jonathan Cape, 1933.
Escape to the Sea by Fred Rebell: John Murray, 1939.
The Venturesome Voyages of Captain Voss by Captain John Voss: John Murray, 1949.
Mosquitoes by William Faulkner: Chatto & Windus, 1964.
The Magic Valley Travellers ed. Peter Haining: Gollancz, 1974.
Welcome to Our District: Official Guide of Deudraeth Rural District.
Edward Wolfe, 1948: Catalogue note to exhibition of paintings.
A Note on the Artist: Edward Wolfe Retrospective Exhibition catalogue, Arts Council, 1967.

Articles

Abbreviations: *G – The Graphic; ES – Evening Standard; L – Listener; NA – The Nation and Athenaeum; NSN – New Statesman and Nation; O – Observer; RT – Radio Times; SRL – Saturday Review of Literature; SWG – Saturday Westminster Gazette; Sp – Spectator; STel – Sunday Telegraph; ST – Sunday Times; T&T – Time and Tide; TLS – Times Literary Supplement; VQR – Virginia Quarterly Review; WWG – Weekly Westminster Gazette; WR – World Review.*

'What's Wrong with the Stage?': *ES,* 5th June 1920.
'Diary of a Steerage Passenger': *SWG,* 19th November 1921, pp.4-5.
'A Diary in Eastern Europe': *WWG,* 9th, 16th, 23rd, 30th September; 7th, 21st October; 4th November, 1922 (in seven parts).
'How Listening Plays are Done': *ES,* 16th January 1924.
'The Cinema's New Rival': *Women's Pictorial,* 29th February 1924.
'Wales and the Welsh': *Review of Reviews,* 15th June 1924, pp.461-466.
'New Trends in the Theatre': *Forum,* June 1925.
'Aspects of the Cinema': *The Outlook,* 2nd January 1926, p.8.
'Under the Nose, Under the Skin': *New York Herald Tribune, Books,* 16th June 1929, pp.1, 6.
'Rum Runners I have Known': *Daily Chronicle and Liverpool Mercury,* 13th December 1929.
'Nightingales and Daggers in Morocco': *RT,* 17th October 1930, pp.161, 180.
'Illogic and the Child': *SRL,* 15th November 1930.
'Strange Christmases': *Harper's Bazaar,* December 1930, pp.75, 96.
'The Relation of Nationalism to Literature': *Transactions of the Honourable Society of Cymmrodorion,* Session 1930-31, pp.107-128.
'My first Day in the Air': *Daily Express,* 20th April 1931.
'Revolution in Tetuan': *G,* 16th May 1931, p.264.
'Under the Nose and Under the Skin': *L,* 10th June 1931, p.979.
'Time to Burn Boats': *Week-End Review,* 10th October 1931, pp.424-425.
'All God's Chillun got Wings': *NSN,* 18th March 1933, pp.321-322.
'Cave Drawings: a New Theory': *NSN,* 1st April 1933, pp.414-415.
'Northern Africa': *L,* 19th April 1933, p.629.
'Notes on the Way': *T&T,* 19.9.36, pp.1273-5; 26.9.36, pp.1306-8; 16.10.37, pp.1361-4; 23.10.37, pp.1393-5; 30.10.37, pp.1428-9; 26.11.38, pp.1638-9; 3.12.38, pp.1686-8; 10.12.38, pp.1778-80; 29.6.40, p.684. 6.7.40, p.708.
'The Gentle Pirate': *L,* 16th June 1938, pp.1268-70.
'Tale-telling for Children': *G,* 16th June 1938, pp.222-223.
'Birth of a Hurricane': *L,* 15th October 1938.
'Will Radio Develop a Literature of its Own?': *WR,* November 1946, pp.33-36.
'The Second Revolution: Literature and Radio': *VQR* XXIII, Winter 1947, pp.34-43.
'The Writer's Duty': *L,* 22nd July 1948, pp.131-132.
'Polish Impressions': *Sp,* 17th September 1948, p.358.
'Star Tiger Down': *Sp,* 8th October 1948, pp.457-458.
'Politicians are Specialists': *Our Time,* vol.17 no.3, October 1948, p.338.
'Make Parenthood Possible': *WR,* December 1949, pp.48-52.
'Robert Louis Stevenson': *L,* 16th November 1950, pp.533-534.
'Wales through the Looking-glass': *L,* 24th May 1951, pp.838-839.

'The Coronation in Wales': *T&T,* June 1953.
'George Borrow: Victorian Rebel': *RT,* 3rd December 1954, p.4.
'The Birth of Radio Drama': *Atlantic Monthly,* December 1957, pp.145-148.
'Last Words from Augustus': *STel,* 5th November 1961.
'Liturgical Language Today': *Province* vol. XIII no.4, 1962. Subsequently published as
   a Church in Wales pamphlet.
'Faulkner and Bennett': *Encounter* XXI:3, September 1963, pp.59-61
'Seven Mirrors for Parishes': *Six Lay Voices,* Church in Wales publications, 1964,
   pp.29-35.
'Poet with Frying-Pan': *STel,* 25th July 1965, p.14.
'African Authors – Read your Contracts!': *Nairobi Nation,* 27th February 1967.
'Fiction as Truth': *Proceedings of the American Academy of Arts and Letters and the National
   Institute of Arts and Letters,* Second Series, no.20, 1970, pp.16-20 ('The Blashfield
   Address').
'Not things, but persons': *Times Saturday Review,* 21st March 1970, p.1.
'You should have been here yesterday': *O,* 17th January 1971, p.24.
'Eheu Fugaces': *VQR* LI, Spring 1975, pp.258-263.

Reviews

The Wisdom of Akhnaton by A.E. Grantham, *Touch and Go* by D.H. Lawrence, *The Powers
of the Air* by Sturge Moore: *SWG,* 28th July 1920.
Collected Poems by Edward Thomas, *A Song of Life and other poems* by W.H. Davies,
Wayside Poems by Gerald Bull: *SWG,* 25th September 1920.
Over the Brazier by Robert Graves, *The Waggoner and other poems* by Edmund Blunden,
The Moon by J.C. Squire: *SWG,* 2nd October 1920.
A Village Sermon by Herbert Asquith, *Poems* by Sir Cecil Spring-Rice: *SWG,*
23rd October 1920.
Aria de Capo by Edna St Vincent Millay, *Otherworld: Cadences* by F.S. Flint, *The Romance of
Youth* by E.E. Bradford, *Poems of Expression* by T.G.W. Henslow: *SWG,*
30th October 1920.
Outlines of Modern English Literature by Harold Williams: *SWG,* 6th November 1920.
Absaloma Tragedy by Torahiko Khori, *The Poet in the Desert* by C.E. Scott Wood, *Songs of the
Cattle Trail and Cow Camp* by John A. Lomax. *To-day and Yesterday* by William Dudley
Foulke, *Hamewith* by Charles Murray: *SWG,* 27th November 1920.
The Collected Prose of James Elroy Flecker: SWG, 12th March 1921.
Pengard Awake by Ralph Straus: *SWG,* 19th March 1921.
'Some notes on W.E. Henley' (Review of three-volume *Collected Works*): *SWG,*
19th March 1921.
Three Plays by Luigi Pirandello: *WWG,* 29th December 1923.
Beasts, Birds and Flowers by D.H. Lawrence: *NA,* 5th January 1924.
Essays on Poetry by J.C. Squire: *WWG,* 19th January 1924.
The Story of My Heart by Richard Jefferies: *WWG,* 2nd February 1924.
Crossings: A Fairy Play by Walter de la Mare. *Sp,* 15th November 1924.
Mrs Dalloway by Virginia Woolf: *SRL,* 16th May 1925.
Messages by Ramon Fernandez: *NA,* 27th August 1927.
Camera Obscura by William Bolitho: *News Chronicle,* 17th June 1931.
Seven Pillars of Wisdom by T.E. Lawrence: *Sp,* 2nd August 1935.
Ships by Hendrik van Loon: *Sp,* 20th December 1935.

Uffa Fox's Second Book by Uffa Fox: *Sp*, 24th January 1936.

Freak Ships by Stanley Rogers; *The History of American Sailing* by Howard I. Chapelle: *Sp*, 24th July 1936.

Flowering Nettle by Harry Martinson: *O*, 4th October 1936.

American Sailing Craft by Howard I. Chapelle; *The Anatomy of Neptune* by Brian Tunstall; *Ships That Have Made History* by Gregory Robinson; *The Flower of England's Garland* by G.E. Mainwaring; *Crimes of the High Seas* by David Masters: *Sp*, 16th October 1936.

The Blue Bed by Glyn Jones: *O*, 7th February 1937.

Sailing and Cruising by K. Adlard Coles; *The King's Britannica* by John Irving; *Clipper Ships of America and Great Britain* by Helen and Jaques la Grange: *NSN*, 26th June 1937.

The Letters of T.E. Lawrence ed. David Garnett: *NSN*, 10th December 1938.

The Beauty of Sail by Uffa Fox; *The Yachtman's Weekend Book* by John Irving and Douglas Service; *Thoughts on Yachts and Yachting* by Uffa Fox; *The Yachtman's Annual and Who's Who: NSN*, 7th January 1939.

The Passing of the Aborigines by Daisy Bates: *ST*, 15th January 1939.

On Sailing the Sea: a Collection of the Seagoing Writings of Hilaire Belloc and W.N. Roughead: *NSN*, 10th February 1940.

Wind Aloft, Wind Alow by Marin-Marie: *ST*, 18th November 1945.

The Buttercup Field and other stories by Gwyn Jones: *TLS*, 30th December 1945.

Time in the East by Evan John; *Jungle Pilot* by Barry Sutton: *ST*, 28th April 1946.

Sailing Through Life by John Scott Hughes: *ST*, 31st August 1947.

The Ashley Book of Knots by Clifford Ashley: *ST*, 16th November 1947.

Sailing Around the World by Capt. Joshua Slocum: *T&T*, 17th April 1948.

Nuremberg Diary by G.M. Gilbert: *ST*, 1st August 1948.

The Kon-Tiki Expedition by Thor Heyerdahl: *O*, 2nd April 1950.

Humanities by Desmond MacCarthy: *Sp*, 2nd October 1953.

The Hill of Devi by E.M. Forster: *Sp*, 16th October 1953.

A Writer's Diary – extracts from the Diary of Virginia Woolf ed. Leonard Woolf: *Sp*, 20th November 1953.

Except the Lord by Joyce Cary: *Sp*, 18th December 1953.

The Golden Horizon ed. Cyril Connolly: *ST*, 20th December 1953.

The Strachey Family by Charles R. Sanders: *Sp*, 5th February 1954.

Under Milk Wood by Dylan Thomas: *ST*, 7th March 1954.

Katherine Mansfield by Anthony Alpers: *ST*, 25th April 1954.

The Memoirs of a Buccaneer by Louis Le Golif: *ST*, 12th May 1954.

The Bloomsbury Group by J.K. Johnstone: *Sp*, 11th June 1954.

The Power of Words by Stuart Chase: *ST*, 15th May 1955.

Double Talk by Harry Hodgkinson: *ST*, 26th June 1955.

Elinor Glyn by Anthony Glyn: *ST*, 24th July 1955.

The Opposing Self by Lionel Trilling: *ST*, 7th August 1955.

Adventures in the Skin Trade by Dylan Thomas: *ST*, 11th September 1955.

A History of Welsh Literature by Thomas Parry; *An Introduction to Welsh Poetry* by Gwyn Williams: *ST*, January 1956.

Gipsy Moth Circles the World by Francis Chichester: *ST*, 12th November 1967.

John Strachey by Hugh Thomas: *ST*, 6th May 1973.